DRE 098: Integrated Reading and Writing III

Wake Technical Community College

Custom Edition

D1307892

CENGAGE
Learning·

Australia • Brazil • Japan • Korea • Mexico • Singapore • Spain • United Kingdom • United States

CENGAGE
Learning

DRE 098: Integrated Reading and Writing III, Wake Technical Community College, Custom Edition

For product information and technology assistance, contact us at
Cengage Learning Customer & Sales Support, 1-800-354-9706
For permission to use material from this text or product,
submit all requests online at **cengage.com/permissions**
Further permissions questions can be emailed to
permissionrequest@cengage.com

This book contains select works from existing Cengage Learning resources and was produced by Cengage Learning Custom Solutions for collegiate use. As such, those adopting and/or contributing to this work are responsible for editorial content accuracy, continuity and completeness.

Compilation © 2014 Cengage Learning
ISBN-13: 978-1-305-29282-6

ISBN-10: 1-305-29282-0

WCN: 01-100-101

Senior Manager, Student Engagement:

Linda deStefano

Janey Moeller

Manager, Student Engagement:

Julie Dierig

Marketing Manager:

Rachael Kloos

Manager, Production Editorial:

Kim Fry

Manager, Intellectual Property Project Manager:

Brian Methe

Senior Manager, Production and Manufacturing:

Donna M. Brown

Manager, Production:

Terri Daley

Cengage Learning

5191 Natorp Boulevard
Mason, Ohio 45040
USA

Cengage Learning is a leading provider of customized learning solutions with office locations around the globe, including Singapore, the United Kingdom, Australia, Mexico, Brazil, and Japan. Locate your local office at:
international.cengage.com/region.

Cengage Learning products are represented in Canada by Nelson Education, Ltd.
For your lifelong learning solutions, visit **www.cengage.com/custom.**
Visit our corporate website at **www.cengage.com.**
Visit signature labs online at **signaturelabs.com.**

Printed in the United States of America

Acknowledgements

The content of this text has been adapted from the following product(s):

Source Title: The Human Cost of an Illiterate Society
ISBN10: 9781285615745

Source Title: The New World Reader
Authors: Muller
ISBN10: 143908338X
ISBN13: 9781439083383

Source Title: National Geographic Learning Reader: Cultural Identity in America
Authors: Learning
ISBN10: 1133946356
ISBN13: 9781133946359

Source Title: The Harbrace Guide to Writing
Authors: Glenn
ISBN10: 1111349096
ISBN13: 9781111349097

Source Title: National Geographic Learning Reader: Living in the World: Cultural Themes for Writers (Book Only)
Authors: National Geographic Learning
ISBN10: 1285422848
ISBN13: 9781285422848

Source Title: Communication in Our Lives

Authors: Wood
ISBN10: 1285075978
ISBN13: 9781285075976

Source Title: How Facebook Is Making Friending Obsolete
ISBN10: 9781285393384

Source Title: Sex, Lies and Conversation: Why Is It So Hard for Men and Women to Talk to Each Other?
ISBN10: 9781285388724

Source Title: Black Men and Public Space
ISBN10: 9781285388717

Source Title: What's in a Word?
ISBN10: 9781285618326

Source Title: Is Google Making Us Stupid?
ISBN10: 9781285393391

Brief Contents

Chapter 1   ZipUSA: New York, NY 10013; "After the Fall" 2

Chapter 2   Hip-Hop Planet 8

Chapter 3   Black Men and Public Space 19

Chapter 4   How Walt Disney Changed Everything 22

Chapter 5   London on a Roll 34

Chapter 6   Communication and Personal Identity 47

Chapter 7   Sex, Lies and Conversation; Why Is It So Hard for Men and
             Women to Talk to Each Other? 71

Chapter 8   Speaking in Tongues: Does Language Unify or Divide Us? 77

Chapter 9   What's in a Word? 117

Chapter 10   The Human Cost of an Illiterate Society 119

Chapter 11   Examining the Millennial Generation: Responding with
             Investigative Reports 127

Chapter 12   How Facebook is Making Friending Obsolete 163

Chapter 13   Is Google Making Us Stupid? 165

Index   173

1

ZipUSA: NEW YORK, NY 10013; "AFTER THE FALL"

A year after the attack on Manhattan's World Trade Center on September 11, 2001, a firefighter and two neighborhood residents recall their experiences on that fateful day and reflect on the effects on their city and their lives.

As you read "After the Fall," you should consider the following questions:

- As you read the three accounts of 9/11, what feelings do you find dominant?
- Which feelings resonate with you?

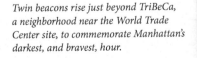

Twin beacons rise just beyond TriBeCa, a neighborhood near the World Trade Center site, to commemorate Manhattan's darkest, and bravest, hour.

2

ZipUSA: NEW YORK CITY, NY 10013; AFTER THE FALL

Photographs by Ira Block

FOUR BLOCKS FROM THE WORLD TRADE CENTER (ZIP CODE 10048) ZIP CODE 10013 BEGINS. THE END OF 10048 IS TOLD BY A FIREFIGHTER

WHOSE HOUSE LOST 14 MEN ON SEPTEMBER 11.

TWO 10013 RESIDENTS FILL OUT THE TALE.

Only hours after the collapse of the towers, the recovery had begun.

CANTO I: After the towers collapse, I arrive on the scene. There are no streets, only caverns of destruction, filled with sections of I beams, aluminum facade, dust, paper, and mud. Buildings surrounding what will come to be known as ground zero are gutted, burning fiercely, have hundreds of broken windows, or have been ripped wide open by flying girders. The command system is shattered; a chief is yelling orders from atop a rig. Every man seems to be from a different unit, and most lack basic equipment. We stretch hose lines to control fires in the acres of rubble, and pass stretchers, breathing masks, and forcible-entry tools over the girders to try to rescue trapped firemen.

Later I find my company, Ladder 15, at a staging area, where they've set up chairs outside the shattered windows of an office building's backside, like some war zone Parisian café.

After a few hours of awaiting orders, we split up to look for work. I find a large contingent of firefighters and police on the south side of Tower 2's remains, snaking a hose line into the rubble's smoky darkness. I search for victims under the wreckage. No sign of anyone.

From time to time the smoke lifts a little, showing six stories of uncollapsed steel girders and concrete flooring looming overhead. I keep searching, making mental notes of what girder I'll duck under if the rest of the building gives way.

Men shout for relief at the end of the hose line. I follow the line into intense heat and choking smoke. About a half hour later I reach the end and offer to take the nozzle, but the nozzleman refuses. "I'm not going anywhere until Duncan comes back!" he yells. By tradition, a company keeps the nozzle until the fire is out and firefighters from the house are safe. I help feed in hose, then start back to get some tools. Suddenly I feel sick and dehydrated. Hundreds of hands steady me as I clamber over rubble and down ladders that the brothers have laid across the steepest sections.

In the triage center in the firehouse across the street, the nurses seem like angels with IVs.

Adapted from "ZipUSA: New York, New York 10013; After the fall" by Noel Maitland: National Geographic Magazine, September 2002.

Before I fall asleep, I think back to the afternoon, when firefighters and construction workers fired up earthmoving equipment and started clearing the street. Only hours after the collapse of the towers, the recovery had begun.

—NOEL MAITLAND

CANTO II: You know my neighborhood. Last September, the sidewalk in front of my home became the backdrop for news reporters showing the world the devastation. My neighborhood, TriBeCa, just north of ground zero, also became a triage center when merchants threw open their doors to the injured and scared. It became a staging area for rescue workers searching for survivors in the smoldering rubble at the end of my street. And my corner was one where thousands streamed to pay final respects to those lost in a national tragedy that played itself out in an American neighborhood.

We had elementary schools and a canine day care center. We were also home to Miramax Films and some of the world's trendiest restaurants. We were an eclectic mix of artists, Wall Street brokers, and middle-class families. We are different now. Weary from the effort to recover and plagued by uncertainty, we are a neighborhood adrift.

Paul, a neighbor, was the son of "homesteaders," middle-class families attracted here by city subsidies after the towers were built in the mid-seventies. Like so many Americans, he decided to raise his own family where he grew up. A month after the attacks, he packed up and left. For how long? I asked. "Forever," he replied.

A friend from uptown offered to walk me home one night. As we walked down my street, he grabbed my arm in alarm. "I know that smell," he said, of the ever present smoke in the night air, reminder of the fires still burning deep inside that diminishing pile. "I grew up next to a cemetery," he

> Last September, the sidewalk in front of my home became the backdrop for news reporters showing the world the devastation.

said. It was the smell of the crematorium.

I watched one morning as a father walked his son to school down my street. Once-proud skyscrapers stood vacant, their facades burned and stripped, their offices charred honeycombs. The son took his father's hand and asked, "Where is the future?" His father replied, "The future is everywhere around you, at all times."

—DIANA KANE

CANTO III: Weeks later, when the sirens had vanished from the night and we were no longer asked for passports, gas bills, and drivers' licenses to prove that we lived in what we came to call the frozen zone, everything looked the same and everything felt different.

My wife, Fukiko, and I were lucky. We had been across the street when Tower 2 came down with the roaring sound of a steel-and-glass avalanche. We were engulfed by that cloud of dust that rose 25 stories above the street, a cloud so opaque that it looked like a solid. The cloud was made of pulverized floors, exploded glass, smashed desks, computers, food, file cabinets, and human beings. She and I were separated in the dust, found our way home separately, and celebrated the simple fact of being alive.

We were lucky in another way: In our loft 14 blocks north of ground zero, we had electricity. Television, telephones, the Internet all worked. So did we. For nine straight days, we wrote newspaper stories about the calamity. On the tenth day I wrote nothing and for the first time sat on a couch, thinking about the ruined world, and wept.

But life also provided its own consolations. In the streets we met some of our neighbors for the first time. We stood on street corners together, manual laborers and dot-com workers, mothers and children, all staring downtown at the smoldering stumps of the towers. We asked about children, and dogs, and survivors. The emotions of awe, horror, rage were gone quickly, replaced by a shared sense of vulnerability.

That is what remains: vulnerability. And from vulnerability there has emerged a tough fatalism. We all learned, that terrible morning, that we could die while reaching for a piece of toast at breakfast. Where I live, that knowledge has made us more human. Even on streets noisy again with traffic, strangers say good morning. Men kiss their wives more, and hug their children, and walk with them to the Hudson to embrace the sunset. But not one talks with utter confidence about tomorrow.

—PETE HAMILL

Discussion Questions:

- How would you characterize each of the three voices in this essay? What distinguishes each one? What do they have in common?

- What lessons do these three New Yorkers take away from 9/11? In what ways might they be applicable more generally?

Writing Activities

- Given that a "canto" is a major division of a long poem, what does the arrangement of the article into three cantos suggest? What does this way of approaching 9/11 imply?

- What are some examples of recovery in this article? What specific senses of the word do they exemplify? As you consider and compare them, develop a definition of what "recovery" means.

Collaborative Activities

- What does living in a "post–9/11" world mean to each of the students in the classroom? Is there any common theme? Consider differences, too, and what their significance might be.

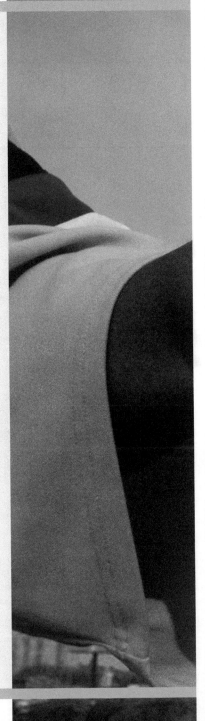

HIP-HOP PLANET

With roots in Africa and the slave trade, and with more recent sources in U.S. ghettoes, such as the South Bronx, hip-hop has become not only a global phenomenon but also a huge and lucrative industry. What makes hip-hop so appealing over time and across cultures, and what makes it so successful commercially are key questions asked by James McBride, a journalist, a jazz musician, and, until recently, an outlier from the "hip-hop planet" he describes.

As you read "Hip-Hop Planet," you should consider the following questions:

- At the beginning of this essay, McBride explicitly acknowledges a generation gap. Does it affect your response to his treatment of hip-hop?
- Similarly, McBride's racial background is also important, as he notes. How might your own figure in your reading of this essay?

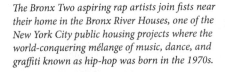

The Bronx Two aspiring rap artists join fists near their home in the Bronx River Houses, one of the New York City public housing projects where the world-conquering mélange of music, dance, and graffiti known as hip-hop was born in the 1970s.

HIP-HOP PLANET

Photographs by David Alan Harvey

AFRICA *Traditional drumming propels a newborn's welcoming ceremony in the Casamance region of Senegal. Powerful West African rhythms survived the slave trade and continue to pulse in the lands of the African diaspora, laying a foundation for many popular music forms: jazz, salsa, rock, hip-hop.*

AUTHOR JAMES MCBRIDE SEARCHES FOR THE

ROOTS OF THE MUSIC

THAT CAN'T BE IGNORED.

I **live on a hip-hop planet.**

This is my nightmare: My daughter comes home with a guy and says, "Dad, we're getting married." And he's a rapper, with a mouthful of gold teeth, a do-rag on his head, muscles popping out his arms, and a thug attitude. And then the nightmare gets deeper, because before you know it, I'm hearing the pitter-patter of little feet, their offspring, cascading through my living room, cascading through my life, drowning me with the sound of my own hypocrisy, because when I was young, I was a knucklehead, too, hearing my own music, my own sounds. And so I curse the day I saw his face, which is a reflection of my own, and I rue the day I heard his name, because I realize to my horror that rap—music seemingly without melody, sensibility, instruments, verse, or harmony, music with no beginning, end, or middle, music that doesn't even seem to be music—rules the world. It is no longer my world. It is his world. And I live in it. I live on a hip-hop planet.

Not since the advent of swing jazz in the 1930s has an American music exploded across the world with such overwhelming force. Not since the Beatles invaded America and Elvis packed up his blue suede shoes has a music crashed against the world with such outrage. This defiant culture of song, graffiti, and dance, collectively known as hip-hop, has ripped popular music from its moorings in every society it has permeated. In Brazil, rap rivals samba in popularity. In China, teens spray-paint graffiti on the Great Wall. In France it has been blamed, unfairly, for the worst civil unrest that country has seen in decades.

Its structure is unique, complex, and at times bewildering. Whatever music it eats becomes part of its vocabulary, and as the commercial world falls into place behind it to gobble up the powerful slop in its wake, it metamorphoses into the Next Big Thing. It is a music that defies definition, yet defines our collective societies in immeasurable ways. To many of my generation, despite all attempts to exploit it, belittle it, numb it, classify it, and analyze it, hip-hop remains an enigma, a clarion call, a cry of "I am" from the youth of the world.

Adapted from "Hip-Hop Planet" by James McBride: National Geographic Magazine, April 2007.

11

We'd be wise, I suppose, to start paying attention.

Hip-hop is a music dipped in the boiling cauldron of race and class, and for that reason it is clouded with mystics, snake oil salesmen, two-bit scholars, race-baiters, and sneaker salesmen, all professing to know the facts, to be "real," when the reality of race is like shifting sand, dependent on time, place, circumstance, and who's telling the history. Here's the real story: In the mid-1970s, New York City was nearly broke. The public school system cut funding for the arts drastically. Gone were the days when you could wander into the band room, rent a clarinet for a minimal fee, and march it home to squeal on it and drive your parents nuts.

The kids of the South Bronx and Harlem came up with something else. In the summer of 1973, at 1595 East 174th Street in the Bronx River Houses, a black teenager named Afrika Bambaataa stuck a speaker in his mother's first-floor living room window, ran a wire to the turntable in his bedroom, and set the housing project of 3,000 people alight with party music. At the same time, a Jamaican teenager named Kool DJ Herc was starting up the scene in the East Bronx, while a technical whiz named Grandmaster Flash was rising to prominence a couple of miles south. The Bronx became a music magnet for Puerto Ricans, Jamaicans, Dominicans, and black Americans from the surrounding areas. Fab 5 Freddy, Kurtis Blow, and Melle Mel were only a few of the pioneers. Grand Wizard Theodore, Kool DJ AJ, the Cold Crush Brothers, Spoony Gee, and the Rock Steady Crew of B-boys showed up to "battle"—dance, trade quips and rhymes, check out each other's records and equipment—not knowing as they strolled through the doors of the community center near Bambaataa's mother's apartment that they were writing musical history. Among them was an MC

The long history is that spoken-word of music made its way here on slave ships from West Africa centuries ago.

named Lovebug Starski, who was said to utter the phrase "hip-hop" between breaks to keep time.

This is how it worked: One guy, the DJ, played records on two turntables. One guy—or girl—served as master of ceremonies, or MC. The DJs learned to move the record back and forth under the needle to create a "scratch," or to drop the needle on the record where the beat was the hottest, playing "the break" over and over to keep the folks dancing. The MCs "rapped" over the music to keep the party going. One MC sought to outchat the other. Dance styles were created —"locking" and "popping" and "breaking." Graffiti artists spread the word of the "I" because the music was all about identity: I am the best. I spread the most love in the Bronx, in Harlem, in Queens. The focus initially was not on the MCs, but on the dancers, or B-boys. Commercial radio ignored it. DJs sold mix tapes out of the back of station wagons. "Rapper's Delight" by the Sugarhill Gang broke the music onto radio in 1979.

That is the short history.

The long history is that spoken-word music made its way here on slave ships from West Africa centuries ago: Ethnomusicologists trace hip-hop's roots to the dance, drum, and song of West African griots, or storytellers, its pairing of word and music the manifestation of the painful journey of slaves who survived the middle passage. The ring shouts, field hollers, and spirituals of early slaves drew on common elements of African music, such as call and response and improvisation. "Speech-song has been part of black culture for a long, long time," says Samuel A. Floyd, director of the Center for Black Music Research at Columbia College in Chicago. The "dozens," "toasts," and "signifying" of black Americans—verbal dueling, rhyming, self-deprecating tales, and stories of blacks outsmarting whites—were defensive, empowering strategies.

Paco Arias (in Cardinals jersey) escaped a world of gangs and violence when he moved from a rough Chicago neighborhood to suburban Dayton. The 14-year-old soon linked up with other teens who share his love of hip-hop, far from the conditions in which it arose.

Highways wrap around the city of Dayton, Ohio, like a ribbon bow-tied on a box of chocolates from the local Esther Price candy factory. They have six ladies at the plant who do just that: Tie ribbons around boxes all day. Henry Rosenkranz can tell you about it. "I love candy," says Henry, a slim white teenager in glasses and a hairnet, as he strolls the factory, bucket in hand. His full-time after-school job is mopping the floors.

Henry is a model American teenager—and the prototypical consumer at which the hip-hop industry is squarely aimed, which has his parents sitting up in their seats. The music that was once the purview of black America has gone white and gone commercial all at once. A sea of white faces now rises up to greet rap groups as they perform, many of them

teenagers like Henry, a NASCAR fanatic and self-described redneck. "I live in Old North Dayton," he says. "It's a white, redneck area. But hip-hop is so prominent with country people … if you put them behind a curtain and hear them talk, you won't know if they're black or white. There's a guy I work with, when Kanye West sings about a gold digger, he can relate because he's paying alimony and child support."

Obviously, it's not just working-class whites, but also affluent, suburban kids who identify with this music with African-American roots. A white 16-year-old hollering rap lyrics at the top of his lungs from the driver's seat of his dad's late-model Lexus may not have the same rationale to howl at the moon as a working-class kid whose parents can't pay for college,

13

yet his own anguish is as real to him as it gets. What attracts white kids to this music is the same thing that prompted outraged congressmen to decry jazz during the 1920s and Tipper Gore to campaign decades later against violent and sexually explicit lyrics: life on the other side of the tracks; its "cool" or illicit factor, which black Americans, like it or not, are always perceived to possess.

Hip-hop has continually changed form, evolving from party music to social commentary with the 1982 release of Grandmaster Flash and the Furious Five's "The Message." Today, alternative hip-hop artists continue to produce socially conscious songs, but most commercial rappers spout violent lyrics that debase women and gays. Beginning with the so-called gangsta rap of the '90s, popularized by the still unsolved murders of rappers Biggie Smalls and Tupac Shakur, the genre has become dominated by rappers who brag about their lives of crime. 50 Cent, the hip-hop star of the moment, trumpets his sexual exploits and boasts that he has been shot nine times.

"People call hip-hop the MTV music now," scoffs Chuck D of Public Enemy, known for its overtly political rap. "It's Big Brother controlling you. To slip something in there that's indigenous to the roots, that pays homage to the music that came before us, it's the Mount Everest of battles."

Most rap songs unabashedly function as walking advertisements for luxury cars, designer clothes, and liquor. Agenda Inc., a "pop culture brand strategy agency" listed Mercedes-Benz as the number one brand mentioned in *Billboard's* top 20 singles in 2005. Hip-hop sells so much Hennessy cognac, listed at number six, that the French makers, deader than yesterday's beer a decade ago, are now rolling in suds. The company

> **E**veryone has the urge deep down to be a bad guy or a bad girl. Everyone likes to talk the talk, but not everyone will walk the walk.

even sponsored a contest to win a visit to its plant in France with a famous rapper.

In many ways, the music represents an old dream. It's the pot of gold to millions of kids like Henry, who quietly agonizes over how his father slaves 14 hours a day at two tool-and-die machine jobs to make ends meet. Like teenagers across the world, he fantasizes about working in the hip-hop business and making millions himself.

"My parents hate hip-hop," Henry says, motoring his 1994 Dodge Shadow through traffic on the way home from work on a hot October afternoon. "But I can listen to Snoop Dogg and hear him call women whores, and I know he has a wife and children at home. It's just a fantasy. Everyone has the urge deep down to be a bad guy or a bad girl. Everyone likes to talk the talk, but not everyone will walk the walk."

You breathe in and breathe out a few times and you are there. Eight hours and a wake-up shake on the flight from New York, and you are on the tarmac in Dakar, Senegal. Welcome to Africa. The assignment: Find the roots of hip-hop. The music goes full circle. The music comes home to Africa. That whole bit. Instead it was the old reporter's joke: You go out to cover a story and the story covers you. The stench of poverty in my nostrils was so strong it pulled me to earth like a hundred-pound ring in my nose. Dakar's Sandaga market is full of "local color"—unless you live there. It was packed and filthy, stalls full of new merchandise surrounded by shattered pieces of life everywhere, broken pipes, bicycle handlebars, fruit flies, soda bottles, beggars, dogs, cell phones. A teenage beggar, his body malformed by polio, crawled by on hands and feet, like a spider. He said, "Hey brother, help me." When I looked into his eyes, they were a bottomless ocean.

In Dakar, where every kid is a microphone and turntable away from squalor, and American rapper Tupac Shakur's picture hangs in market stalls of folks who don't understand English, rap is king. There are hundreds of rap groups in Senegal today. French television crews troop in and out of Dakar's nightclubs filming the kora harp lute and *tama* talking drum with regularity. But beneath the drumming and the dance lessons and the jingling sound of tourist change, there is a quiet rage, a desperate fury among the Senegalese, some of whom seem to bear an intense dislike of their former colonial rulers.

"We know all about French history," says Abdou Ba, a Senegalese producer and musician. "We know about their kings, their castles, their art, their music. We know everything about them. But they don't know much about us."

Assane N'Diaye, 19, loves hip-hop music. Before he left his Senegalese village to work as a DJ in Dakar, he was a fisherman, just like his father, like his father's father before him. Tall, lean, with a muscular build and a handsome chocolate face, Assane became a popular DJ, but the equipment he used was borrowed, and when his friend took it back, success eluded him. He has returned home to Toubab Dialaw, about 25 miles south of Dakar, a village marked by a huge boulder, perhaps 40 feet high, facing the Atlantic Ocean.

About a century and a half ago, a local ruler led a group of people fleeing slave traders to this place. He was told by a white trader to come here, to Toubab Dialaw. When he arrived, the slavers followed. A battle ensued. The ruler fought bravely but was killed. The villagers buried him by the sea and marked his grave with a small stone, and over the years it is said to have sprouted like a tree planted by God. It became a huge, arching boulder that stares out to sea, protecting the village behind it. When the fishermen went deep out to sea, the boulder was like a lighthouse that marked

the way home. The Great Rock of Toubab Dialaw is said to hold a magic spirit, a spirit that Assane N'Diaye believes in.

In the shadow of the Great Rock, Assane has built a small restaurant, Chez Las, decorated with hundreds of seashells. It is where he lives his hip-hop dream. At night, he and his brother and cousin stand by the Great Rock and face the sea. They meditate. They pray. Then they write rap lyrics that are worlds away from the bling-bling culture of today's commercial hip-hoppers. They write about their lives as village fishermen, the scarcity of catch forcing them to fish in deeper and deeper waters, the hardship of fishing for 8, 10, 14 days at a time in an open pirogue in rainy season, the high fee they pay to rent the boat, and the paltry price their catches fetch on the market. They write about the humiliation of poverty, watching their town sprout up around them with rich Dakarians and richer French. And they write about the relatives who leave in the morning and never return, surrendered to the sea, sharks, and God.

The dream, of course, is to make a record. They have their own demo, their own logo, and their own name, Salam T. D. (for Toubab Dialaw). But rap music represents a deeper dream: a better life. "We want money to help our parents," Assane says over dinner. "We watch our mothers boil water to cook and have nothing to put in the pot."

He fingers his food lightly. "Rap doesn't belong to American culture," he says. "It belongs here. It has always existed here, because of our pain and our hardships and our suffering."

Some call the Bronx River Houses the City of Gods, though if God has been by lately, he must've slipped out for a chicken sandwich. The 10 drab, red-brick buildings spread out across 14 acres, coming into view as you drive east across the East 174th Street Bridge. The Bronx is the hallowed holy ground of hip-hop, the place where it all began. Visitors take tours

15

Hip-hop comes full circle on a beach outside Dakar. Jally, a kora-playing griot who makes a living telling stories at ritual ceremonies (or for tourists), jams with Omar N'Gala Seck, a rapper who infuses the American form with fresh shots of its African roots.

through this neighborhood now, care of a handful of fortyish "old-timers," who point out the high and low spots of hip-hop's birthplace.

It is a telling metaphor for the state of America's racial landscape that you need a permit to hold a party in the same parks and playgrounds that produced the music that changed the world. The rap artists come and go, but the conditions that produced them linger. Forty percent of New York City's black males are jobless. One in three black males born in 2001 will end up in prison. The life expectancy of black men in the U.S. ranks below that of men in Sri Lanka and Colombia. It took a massive hurricane in New Orleans for the United States to wake up to its racial realities.

That is why, after 26 years, I have come to embrace this music I tried so hard to ignore. Hip-hop culture is not mine. Yet I own it.

Much of it I hate. Yet I love it, the good of it. To confess a love for a music that, at least in part, embraces violence is no easy matter, but then again our national anthem talks about bombs bursting in air, and I love that song, too. At its best, hip-hop lays bare the empty moral cupboard that is our generation's legacy. This music that once made visible the inner culture of America's greatest social problem, its legacy of slavery, has taken the dream deferred to a global scale. Today, 2 percent of the Earth's adult population owns more than 50 percent of its household wealth, and indigenous cultures are swallowed with the rapidity of a teenager gobbling a bag of potato chips. The music is calling. Over the years, the instruments change, but the message is the same. The drums are pounding out a warning. They are telling us something. Our children can hear it.

The question is: Can we?

Discussion Questions:

- What makes hip-hop a uniting force--and for whom? How can it also be divisive--and in what ways?

- What happens when countercultural phenomena such as hip-hop go mainstream? Does the sting get dulled? Does complicity in the institutions and conditions that hip-hop critiques invalidate the message?

- In what ways does hip-hop transcend racial differences, especially in the United States? In what ways does it reinforce and even exploit these differences? Which tendency seems more prominent? More significant? Why?

- While one crucible of hip-hop is the South Bronx, another is Senegal. How does McBride navigate between the two? What does hip-hop's becoming such a global phenomenon further suggest?

Writing Activities

- "Hip-hop remains an enigma," says McBride, and yet it is also "all about identity." How are the two statements contradictory? How are they complementary?

- Do you consider yourself a member of the "hip-hop planet"? If so, what draws you to it, and what do you gain from it? If not, why not? And what are the ramifications?

- "'It's just a fantasy,'" says one young man of the glorification of violence, crime, and sexual abuse that some of the more popular and commercially successful hip-hop conveys. Do you agree? And even if it is mere fantasy, is it necessarily innocuous when it comes to the real world?

- Concluding the essay by re-emphasizing the importance of hip-hop to a generation younger than his, McBride says the music is "telling us something. Our children can hear it." Do you yourself hear it? What might that something be? How might you convey the message to your elders--if at all?

Collaborative Activities

- Choose several examples of hip-hop music as a class, divide into groups accordingly, discuss the lyrics and the rhythms of your group's sample, and then compare notes amongst yourselves and in relation to the "hip-hop planet."

- What two or three songs are at the top of the charts in your world today? What genre(s) do these fall into? What do you think accounts for their popularity?

BRENT STAPLES

Brent Staples (1951–) was born in Chester, Pennsylvania, and graduated from Widener University in 1973. He received a doctorate in psychology from the University of Chicago in 1982. After writing for several Chicago publications, he joined the New York Times *in 1985 and became a member of its editorial board in 1990. He has also contributed articles to* Ms. *and* Harper's. *In 1994 he published a memoir,* Parallel Time: Growing Up in Black and White, *recalling a childhood of poverty and violence; he began and ended the book with examinations of his brother's drug-related murder.*

The following essay first appeared in Ms. *in 1986 in a slightly different format and under the title "Just Walk on By." The revised version under the current title was first printed in* Harper's *in 1987.*

Black Men and Public Space *(1986)*

My first victim was a woman—white, well-dressed, probably in her early twenties. I came upon her late one evening on a deserted street in Hyde Park, a relatively affluent neighborhood in an otherwise mean, impoverished section of Chicago. As I swung onto the avenue behind her, there seemed to be a discreet, uninflammatory distance between us. Not so. She cast back a worried glance. To her, the youngish black man—a broad 6 feet 2 inches with a beard and billowing hair, both hands shoved into the pockets of a bulky military jacket—seemed menacingly close. After a few more quick glimpses, she picked up her pace and was soon running in earnest. Within seconds she disappeared into a cross street.

That was more than a decade ago. I was 22 years old, a graduate student newly arrived at the University of Chicago. It was in the echo of that terrified woman's footfalls that I first began to know the unwieldy inheritance I'd come into—the ability to alter public space in ugly ways. It was clear that she thought herself the quarry of a mugger, a rapist, or worse. Suffering a bout of insomnia, however, I was stalking sleep, not defenseless wayfarers. As a softy who is scarcely able to take a knife to a raw chicken—let alone hold one to a person's throat—I was surprised, embarrassed, and dismayed all at once. Her flight made me feel like an accomplice in tyranny. It also made it clear that I was indistinguishable from the muggers who occasionally seeped into the area from the surrounding ghetto. That first encounter, and those that followed, signified that a vast, unnerving gulf lay between nighttime pedestrians— particularly women—and me. And I soon gathered that being perceived as dangerous is a hazard in itself. I only needed to turn a corner into a dicey situation, or crowd some frightened, armed person in a foyer somewhere, or make an errant move after being pulled over by a policeman. Where fear and weapons meet—and they often do in urban America—there is always the possibility of death.

In that first year, my first away from my hometown, I was to become thoroughly familiar with the language of fear. At dark, shadowy intersections, I could cross in front of a car stopped at a traffic light and elicit the *thunk, thunk, thunk, thunk* of the driver—black, white, male, or female—hammering down the door locks. On less traveled streets after dark, I grew accustomed to but never comfortable with people crossing to the other side of the street rather than pass me. Then there were the standard unpleasantries with policemen, doormen, bouncers, cabdrivers, and others whose business it is to screen out troublesome individuals *before* there is any nastiness.

I moved to New York nearly two years ago and I have remained an avid night walker. In central Manhattan, the near-constant crowd cover minimizes tense one-on-one street encounters. Elsewhere—in SoHo, for example, where sidewalks are narrow and tightly spaced buildings shut out the sky— things can get very taut indeed.

5   After dark, on the warrenlike streets of Brooklyn where I live, I often see women who fear the worst from me. They seem to have set their faces on neutral, and with their purse straps strung across their chests bandolier style, they forge ahead as though bracing themselves against being tackled. I understand, of course, that the danger they perceive is not a hallucination. Women are particularly vulnerable to street violence, and young black males are drastically overrepresented among the perpetrators of that violence. Yet these truths are no solace against the kind of alienation that comes of being ever the suspect, a fearsome entity with whom pedestrians avoid making eye contact.

It is not altogether clear to me how I reached the ripe old age of 22 without being conscious of the lethality nighttime pedestrians attributed to me. Perhaps it was because in Chester, Pennsylvania, the small, angry industrial town where I came of age in the 1960s, I was scarcely noticeable against a backdrop of gang warfare, street knifings, and murders. I grew up one of the good boys, had perhaps a half-dozen fistfights. In retrospect, my shyness of combat has clear sources.

As a boy, I saw countless tough guys locked away; I have since buried several, too. They were babies, really—a teenage cousin, a brother of 22, a childhood friend in his mid-twenties—all gone down in episodes of bravado played out in the streets. I came to doubt the virtues of intimidation early on. I chose, perhaps unconsciously, to remain a shadow—timid, but a survivor.

The fearsomeness mistakenly attributed to me in public places often has a perilous flavor. The most frightening of these confusions occurred in the late 1970s and early 1980s, when I worked as a journalist in Chicago. One day, rushing into the office of a magazine I was writing for with a deadline story in hand, I was mistaken for a burglar. The office manager called security and, with an ad hoc posse, pursued me through the labyrinthine halls, nearly to my editor's door. I had no way of proving who I was. I could only move briskly toward the company of someone who knew me.

Another time I was on assignment for a local paper and killing time before an interview. I entered a jewelry store on the city's affluent Near North Side. The proprietor excused herself and returned with an enormous red Doberman pinscher straining at the end of a leash. She stood, the dog extended toward me, silent to my questions, her eyes bulging nearly out of her head. I took a cursory look around, nodded, and bade her good night.

Relatively speaking, however, I never fared as badly as another black male 10 journalist. He went to nearby Waukegan, Illinois, a couple of summers ago to work on a story about a murderer who was born there. Mistaking the reporter for the killer, police officers hauled him from his car at gunpoint and but for his press credentials would probably have tried to book him. Such episodes are not uncommon. Black men trade tales like this all the time.

Over the years, I learned to smother the rage I felt at so often being taken for a criminal. Not to do so would surely have led to madness. I now take precautions to make myself less threatening. I move about with care, particularly late in the evening. I give a wide berth to nervous people on subway platforms during the wee hours, particularly when I have exchanged business clothes for jeans. If I happen to be entering a building behind some people who appear skittish, I may walk by, letting them clear the lobby before I return, so as not to seem to be following them. I have been calm and extremely congenial on those rare occasions when I've been pulled over by the police.

And on late-evening constitutionals I employ what has proved to be an excellent tension-reducing measure: I whistle melodies from Beethoven and Vivaldi and the more popular classical composers. Even steely New Yorkers hunching toward nighttime destinations seem to relax, and occasionally they even join in the tune. Virtually everybody seems to sense that a mugger wouldn't be warbling bright, sunny selections from Vivaldi's *Four Seasons*. It is my equivalent of the cowbell that hikers wear when they know they are in bear country.

4

HOW WALT DISNEY CHANGED EVERYTHING

While millions of tourists throng through Disney World, the theme park is more than just a vacation destination. As T. D. Allman demonstrates, not only did Walt Disney's enterprise radically affect the physical, social, and economic landscape of central Florida, his "Magic Kingdom" also set a precedent for the exurbs that sprawl all over the country and the forces of franchising that influence so much of American culture today.

As you read "How Walt Disney Changed Everything," you should consider the following questions:

- Before reading the article, think about some ideas and/or experiences that the "World of Walt Disney" conjures up for you. As you read on, do you find that your perspective corresponds with the author's?
- After you've read the essay, do you want to go to Orlando? Do you feel as though you're already there?

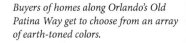

Buyers of homes along Orlando's Old Patina Way get to choose from an array of earth-toned colors.

HOW WALT DISNEY CHANGED EVERY-THING

Photographs by David Burnett

For 13-year-olds Paige Phillips, left, and Abbey Key, of Oxford, Alabama, Disney World is a once-in-a-childhood pilgrimage, a dream come true. Seventy million people a year visit Orlando theme parks.

ORLANDO IS THE NEW AMERICAN METROPOLIS.

Everything happening to America today is happening here, and it's far removed from the cookie-cutter suburbanization of life a generation ago. The Orlando region has become Exhibit A for the ascendant power of our cities' exurbs: blobby coalescences of look-alike, overnight, amoeba-like concentrations of population far from city centers. These huge, sprawling communities are where more and more Americans choose to be, the place where job growth is fastest, home building is briskest, and malls and megachurches are multiplying as newcomers keep on coming. Who are all these people? They're you, they're me, and increasingly, they are nothing like the blue-eyed "Dick and Jane" of mythical suburban America.

Orlando's explosion is visible in every shopping mall and traffic jam. You can also see it from outer space. When Earth satellites were first launched, Florida photographed at night looked like two l's standing side by side: One long string of lights ran down the Atlantic side of the peninsula; another ran along the Gulf of Mexico side. In between was darkness. Today the two parallel l's have become a lopsided *H*. Central Florida glows as though a phosphorescent creature from outer space has landed there and started reproducing. It gobbles up existing communities even as it transforms scrub and swamp into a characterless conurbation of congested freeways and parking lots. All of this is "Orlando," the brand name for this region of two million residents.

When people tell the story of Orlando's stunning transformation from swamp and sinkhole to 21st-century metropolis, they begin, inevitably, with the man and the mouse. The mouse is Mickey, the man Walt Disney. If it weren't for Disney, the local saying goes, the Orlando region would be called Ocala, a rival town up the road. Disney first flew over central Florida in an airplane chartered under an alias to keep his mission

> **O**rlando's explosion is visible in every shopping mall and traffic jam. You can also see it from outer space.

Adapted from "How Walt Disney Changed Everything" by T.D. Allman: National Geographic Magazine, March 2007.

In Red Lobster's test kitchen—birthplace of popcorn shrimp—dishes are tasted again and again en route from the Orlando corporate headquarters to menus at 682 locations nationwide. "We ask, 'Does it move our brand forward?'" says corporate chef Michael LaDuke, third from left.

secret. It was the fateful day of November 22, 1963. The Kennedy assassination would mark America forever. So would the decision Walt Disney made that day to turn an inland Florida agricultural center into an epicenter of world tourism.

Orlando was the county seat of Orange County, but it wasn't citrus groves that prompted Disney's secret aerial reconnaissance. During his flyover, he focused on a wasteland southwest of Orlando where alligators outnumbered people. Porous limestone underlay the vegetal muck. What passed for dry land was speckled with shallow, brown-watered catchments, some the size of station wagons, others the size of suburbs. "That's it," Disney proclaimed,

pointing down to the future site of what he dreamed of creating in this Florida wilderness: Epcot, America's Experimental Prototype Community of Tomorrow.

Over the next two years, with the collusion of Orlando's top leaders, Disney secretly acquired more than 25,000 acres. People were glad to sell dirt cheap. This sludgy terrain was useless for agriculture. It was far from Florida's beaches. It was hot and muggy most of the year, yet it got so cold during central Florida's brief winters that deep freezes periodically killed the citrus crop.

Who would want to vacation in such a place? Disney was certain most Americans would, once he worked his marketing magic on them. By the 1960s, all over America, suburbs were replacing old neighborhoods. Malls were driving Main Street out of business. There was hardly a new ranch home or split-level that didn't have a TV antenna on the roof. Disney realized that in the coming decades shows like *The Mickey Mouse Club,* not climate and geology, would determine what the majority of Americans would consider a safe and enjoyable place to take a family vacation. That day, flying over central Florida, Disney decided that he, not reality, would define what constituted the Magic Kingdom in the minds and spending habits of millions of Americans in the years to come.

The interstate highway system, started by the Eisenhower Administration as part of the Cold War defense effort against communism, was already crisscrossing America. Disney chose Orlando because it was at the confluence of two of the most important of these new thoroughfares, what today are Interstate 4 and Florida's Turnpike. There was also a deeply personal reason he located Disney World there—the same one that still lures people to Orlando today. In Florida's boggy, buggy, empty midsection, Walt Disney perceived a second chance.

His original theme park—Disneyland, in southern California—covered fewer than 300 acres. It soon was ringed with the suburban blight that its success inevitably attracted—motels, strip malls, copycat amusement parks. Disney never forgave himself for not making Disneyland big enough, but in Florida he hoped to rectify that mistake. He set out to create an Adventureland where nothing was left to chance. Arriving visitors would not be permitted to choose their own parking spaces; smiling Disney characters would do that for them. In this new, bigger, better Magic Kingdom, water could not be the tannic brown common in central Florida. So Bay Lake was drained, the sludge removed, and clear water pumped into the resulting lagoon. Even dry land would be turned into another Disney illusion: As you traverse the theme park, you are actually walking on the roof of

an immense, underground control building from which the operation is run, staffed, and supplied.

Disney's new empire in central Florida would be marketed as Disney World. Its official name was, and remains, the Reedy Creek Improvement District. Thanks to a sweetheart deal with the state legislature, the lands Disney purchased were detached from the rest of Florida to form a Magic Kingdom, above and outside the law. Even now, Disney World's rides are exempt from state safety inspections. Democratic process is excluded, too. Power remains in the hands of a board of supervisors composed of Disney allies. However much you pay for a time-share condo in Disney World, you cannot buy property outright, and therefore establish official residence, and therefore vote for the board. Celebration, Disney's residential community themed to evoke pre-1940s small-town America, has a city hall but no actual municipal government.

In this place of exurban, postmodern pioneers, the range of choices is vast even when the choices themselves are illusory. Here life is truly a style: You don't want to live in a mass-produced, instant "community"? No problem. Orlando's developers, like the producers of instant coffee, offer you a variety of flavors, including one called Tradition. Structurally it may seem identical to all the others. Only instead of vaguely Mediterranean ornamental details, the condos at Tradition have old colonial finishes. In Orlando's lively downtown, it's possible to live in a loft just as you would in Chicago or New York. But these lofts are brand-new buildings constructed for those who want the postindustrial lifestyle in a place that never was industrial.

Orlando's bright lights are not the garish displays of Las Vegas or the proud power logos of New York. Instead, Orlando glimmers with the familiar signage of franchise America: Denny's, Burger King, Quality Inn, Hampton Inn, Hertz. Orlando also leads in the culinary transformation of the exotic into the familiar. From its Orlando headquarters, the Darden Corporation, the city's first *Fortune* 500 company, mass-markets theme foods. It standardizes the output of Red Lobsters and Olive Gardens everywhere.

All over Orlando you see forces at work that are changing America from Fairbanks to Little Rock. This, truly, is a 21st-century paradigm: It is growth built on consumption, not production; a society founded not on natural resources, but upon the dissipation of capital accumulated elsewhere; a place of infinite possibilities, somehow held together, to the extent it is held together at all, by a shared recognition of highway signs, brand names, TV shows, and personalities, rather than any shared history. Nowhere else is the juxtaposition of what America actually is and the conventional idea of what America should be more vivid and revealing.

Welcome to the theme-park nation.

Very few people, as they talk about the immense changes reshaping Orlando and their lives, mention another American genius who left his mark here even before Disney arrived. Jack Kerouac—guru, bad boy, the literary superstar who wrote the Beat Generation's manifesto, *On The Road*—came to Orlando, by bus, in December 1956. The following year, in an 11-day creative frenzy, he wrote *The Dharma Bums* in an apartment with a tangerine tree out back, shoveling the words through his typewriter in the heart of hot, flat Florida.

Kerouac's tumultuous vision was a howling rant against the plastic shackles he perceived imprisoning the human spirit in mid-century America. Looking out his window at the neighbors, he scorned "the middle-class non-identity which finds its perfect expression ... in rows of well-to-do houses with lawns and television sets in each living room with

> **A**round the world, Orlando is synonymous with the theme-park culture that has overtaken America.

everybody looking at the same thing and thinking the same thing at the same time." Whereas Disney was looking for control, Kerouac personified the American urge to defy control. Disney acted out the old American idea that if you can just grab hold of enough American wilderness, you can create a world free of the problems that besiege people in places like the frost belt. Kerouac evoked a rootless America where, no matter how far people wander, they never reach their destination.

Never were two men so totally American and so totally different, yet both of them wound up in Orlando. This prophetic convergence raises the question: When it came to America's future, who was the better prophet of what, since then, we and our country have become? As a people, and as a nation, are we more like Disney's smiling "characters"? Or do we more resemble half-lost wanderers, like Kerouac and his crew?

The answer seems clear: Around the world, Orlando is synonymous with the theme-park culture that has overtaken America. Nowhere else does the triumph of the Disney ethos seem so total, yet something paradoxical emerges when you get to know the place. Fifty years on, Kerouac's restless spirit is still on the loose in Orlando's discount shopping malls. It prowls the RV parks and hangs out at the fast-food franchises. Wherever people neglect to mow the grass, or curse the car payments, you're in Kerouac's Orlando because they, like him, were once from someplace else. And, for a while at least, Orlando seemed to them, as it did to the Beat apostle, like a place where the utility bills never get past due and the past can never haunt you.

"Why not come to Orlando and dig the crazy Florida scene of spotlessly clean highways and fantastic supermarkets?" Kerouac wrote Lawrence Ferlinghetti, the Beat poet, in 1961. But in Orlando, as everywhere else he

Streetlamps mark the future homes of Savannah Landings, a development on Orlando's east edge where town houses named Scarlett and Ashley will go for $236,000 and up. Best perk in a far-flung city with no trains and few buses: easy access to Route 417.

roamed, Kerouac never did find escape. Florida became for him, after he stopped writing, a place to drink, and ultimately a place to die. The little house at 1418 Clouser Avenue where Kerouac wrote his novel now serves as a kind of literary time-share, where writers spend three months at a stint, hoping to channel Kerouac's manic genius.

Things did not turn out as Walt Disney intended either. People thronged to the Magic Kingdom to see with their own eyes what they'd seen on TV, but Epcot, Disney's cherished project of creating a futuristic community where people lived and worked in high-tech harmony, never became a reality. People weren't interested in Disney's edgeless version of tomorrow. Epcot was such a failure that Disney officials faced the embarrassing prospect of shutting it down. Instead, they turned it into another tourist attraction. Today

Epcot offers a nostalgic pastiche of a 1940s seashore vacation 60 miles from the nearest sea, along with food options themed to places like Gay Paree, a space ride, and "Key West" time-share options.

By trying to create a Magic Kingdom immune from squalor and complexity, Disney touched off an orgy of uncontrolled growth that still shows no signs of abating. Extinct theme parks litter the Orlando landscape the way dead factories mark the rust belt. Defunct attractions like Splendid China, which featured a miniature Great Wall, went bankrupt because they were too realistic. They failed to provide what all successful theme parks must: fantasies conforming exactly to what the paying public expects to get.

Today Orlando is a cauldron of all the communal characteristics Disney sought to control. In its Parramore district, you can stock up on crack, meth, and angel dust. According to the Morgan Quitno research firm, in 2006 it joined such cities as Detroit and St. Louis to become one of the 25 most dangerous cities in America. The result is armed guards at the gates of "communities" where entry is solely by invitation. The Orlando area also has one of the highest pedestrian death rates among the largest metro regions in the country. Four decades after Disney's fateful flyover, Orlando is a place of enormous vitality, diversity, ugliness, discord, inventiveness, possibility, and disappointed hopes, where no clown in a character costume can tell people how to live, let alone where to park.

These days Orlando is as multicultural as New York, and as much in the throes of globalization as any import-export center. Its growth has brought people speaking more than 70 languages to central Florida. Kissimmee, south of Orlando and just east of Disney World, has gone from being a cowboy town to mostly Hispanic in less than ten years. The tentacles of diversity have penetrated Disney World too. Few tourists realize it, but when their kids hug Goofy and Minnie they might be embracing low-wage workers from places like Sri Lanka and the Dominican Republic.

Some complain the newcomers from developing countries aren't "real Americans." Others complain the newcomers from up north aren't "real Floridians." "We have drive-by citizens," says Linda Chapin, a former Orange County commissioner. People move to Florida, but they don't bring their loyalties with them. In such a situation of psychological rootlessness and moral detachment, the question isn't whether the problems arising from unchecked growth can be solved. It's whether there is any chance of them being addressed at all.

"We've allowed Florida to be turned into a strip mall," says Chapin. "This is our great

> **W**e've allowed Florida to be turned into a strip mall. This is our great tragedy.

tragedy." While she was head of the county commission, she played a major role in unleashing Orlando's nonstop building boom. She masterminded Orlando's new convention center, along with other projects intended to assure an influx of people into the area. "My name is in gold letters over at the convention center," she says. "It makes my mother proud." These days, as head of urban planning at the University of Central Florida, she thinks up ways to slow down Orlando's growth, and humanize it.

Chapin talks about the reasons why, back in the beginning, change and growth seemed like such unalloyed blessings. "We thought we could manage growth," she says. In her lifetime, a sky's-the-limit scenario has turned Orlando into a city of suburban, and human, dilemmas. Still, this is can-do America. As Chapin, suddenly reverting to optimism, puts it: "Just because we've ruined 90 percent of everything doesn't mean we can't do wonderful things with the remaining ten percent!"

You can see Orlando's sprawl from outer space. Go to Cypress Creek High and Meadow Woods Middle School, and you see the human complexity in the eyes of its students. The sky was streaked dawn pink as I headed out to the moving edge of Orlando. Fifteen miles southwest of downtown, I reached the latest spot where central Florida's population explosion has turned wilderness into tract housing overnight. If the moon were ever settled, this is how it would be done. Whole neighborhoods, consisting of hundreds of houses, arrived here instantly. So have the people who live in them.

Demographically, these two schools match the Orlando area. Here both whites and blacks are in the minority; "other" is the dominant ethnicity. I picked them because they are typical schools, but when I visited I found

Debate students at Orlando's Cypress Creek High speak six languages besides English—Hindi, Gujarati, Urdu, Mandarin, Japanese, and Creole. As immigrants pass up gateway cities like Miami for better schools and affordable homes, suburbs are no longer homogenous enclaves.

something extraordinary—two places where more than 8,000 students and teachers were finding new ways to learn, and new ways to live together.

At Cypress Creek and Meadow Woods, great events are not just things these kids and their teachers see on TV. They impinge on people's lives. At Cypress Creek, the assistant principal, Vanessa Colon Schaefer, was still putting her life back together after more than a year in Iraq. When her National Guard unit was sent there, she left a gap in the life of her daughter, and of this school. Kids from nearly 200 countries study at the two schools. "Normally they shout out their countries when I ask them," says Chuck Rivers, the principal at Meadow Woods. "But

one time a little boy just whispered. When I asked him again, he kept whispering, so I bent down to hear him. He whispered 'Iraq' in my ear." Rivers adds, with no false sentimentality, "They're all my kids."

I talk to students from Colombia, Brazil, Haiti, Jamaica, Korea, China, the Philippines, Iran, Russia, Slovakia, and India—and I've just begun to plumb the mutations. "My mother is from Germany," one little girl says, "and my father is from Madagascar." Diversity is not an objective, or a program, or a lifestyle here. It is life.

At Cypress Creek I talk with the school's National Merit Scholars. I visit classes where kids are autistic or deaf or otherwise different. I sense how important it is for children to find themselves integrated, every day, with kids who are different from them mentally, physically, racially, culturally. The principal of Cypress Creek is a woman; the principal of Meadow Woods is black. He remembers the days of racial segregation. Now he is in charge of a learning experience where racial barriers aren't the only things that have become meaningless. No dumbing down is going on here. At the middle school, kids are studying things I never learned in all my years of schooling: how to conduct a symphony, how blood circulates, how to fix a faucet, how to solve disputes openly and nonviolently. As we leave, the principal says something that sticks in my mind: "We do this every day."

One morning i have what people in Orlando call the I-4 experience. I zoom off in my car for a midday appointment. It turns into an afternoon appointment by the time I get there. For most of an hour, every car sits motionless. For the first time I truly understand what people mean when they call I-4 "Orlando's parking lot." Nothing is more obvious than the need for a light-rail system connecting Disney, downtown, the airport, and points in between. But in Orlando people love their cars as much as they hate paying taxes. Orlando's roads, so recently slashed through the wilderness, are already deteriorating.

Being stuck in traffic gives you time to think; I wind up thinking about how different Orlando's image of itself is from reality. The irony of Orlando is that people go there in search of Disneyesque tranquillity—and by doing so, they've unleashed upon the place all the rootless, restless contradictions of America. Here is big city traffic, big city crime, yet people in Orlando cherish the idea that they have escaped the trials people face in other cities. On this morning, it is cold, so cold I turn the car heater to high—though at most times of year it is stultifyingly hot. Ahead of me is an overpass, and just to complete the refutation of Orlando's all-American self-image, a big semi lunges across the overpass. "Lucky Noodles," giant red characters proclaim, both in English and Chinese; it is carrying supplies for Orlando's Asian supermarkets.

For some reason the truck with the graceful Chinese writing on it reminds me of the lyrics of that old Disney theme song:

When you wish upon a star
Makes no difference who you are
Anything your heart desires
Will come to you.

"If your heart is in your dream," the song goes on to allege, "No request is too extreme."

Discussion Questions

- What was Disney's vision for Orlando? How was it realized? How have the ensuing growth and development of Orlando conformed to his plans? How have they diverged?

- What are some of the striking words and images associated with nature in this article and how do they contribute to broader thematic conflicts such as control versus contingency or fantasy versus reality?

- Why was the residential scheme of America's Experimental Prototype Community of Tomorrow (Epcot) a failure? At the same time, even though people did not choose to live there, can the scheme be said to have been in some ways successful?

- In discussing forces of homogenization versus those of diversification, both in Orlando and in the broader American landscape, what kinds of evidence does Allman bring to bear to illustrate these tendencies? Does the article suggest that one or the other is stronger? How and why?

Writing Activities

- Pointing to the growing population of exurban dwellers, Allman asks, "Who are all these people?" and answers, "They're you. They're me." How would you yourself reply to Allman's assertion?

- After juxtaposing Jack Kerouac and Walt Disney, Allman wonders, "When it came to America's future, who was the better prophet of what, since then, we and our country have become? As a people, and as a nation, are we more like Disney's smiling 'characters'? Or do we more resemble half-lost wanderers, like Kerouac and his crew?" What would you say?

- Compare the place where you grew up—whether in the country or in the city, in a village or town, in suburbia or exurbia, in the United States or elsewhere—with that of Orlando. Are there any striking similarities and/or differences? What might some of the implications be?

- What do you make of Allman's observation that Disney World is "an adventureland where nothing [is] left up to chance"? As you analyze the meaning and implications of this phrase, consider whether and to what extent other features of American culture exemplify this quality.

Collaborative Activities

- "Life, liberty, and the pursuit of happiness": Does Disney World exemplify these American principles, or undermine them?

- Using the Internet, identify three or four major attractions at Disney World and divide them among study groups. After each group learns as much as possible about its topic—including perhaps taking a virtual tour—each should consider what is, and is not, attractive about the chosen feature. Then, groups can compare notes, as well as further thoughts about the nature of the appeal of Disney World.

5 LONDON ON A ROLL

By Simon Worrall

Photographs by Jodi Cobb

LONDON ON A ROLL

London is the most populous city in the European Union, as well as one of the largest. It's been called a "Leviathan" and a "Babylon;" either way, its vitality is unmistakable. As Samuel Johnson said, "When a man is tired of London, he is tired of life; for there is in London all that life can afford." The observation holds just as true now as it was two hundred years ago. Produced by journalist Simon Worrall and photographer Jodi Cobb, both of whom might be termed world citizens, this feature article shows "London on a Roll," remaking itself as it always has as a world city and creating a thriving urban culture for the 21st century.

Aerial view of London showing Big Ben, the Houses of Parliament, and Westminster Abbey lining the banks of the River Thames. London is a "messy and confusing city," writes historian Stephen Inwood. Yet the disheveled grande dame of the Thames is enjoying a building boom unparalleled since recovery from World War II.

Preening is a serious pastime for London's "It girls"—beauties like Alexandra Aitken who serve as fashionable and ubiquitous adornments on the party circuit. "They're world famous in London," jokes one public relations agent. In its way, the town Dickens quaintly called a "magic lantern" has become "It" among global cities, beaming with the intensity of a socialite's smile.

SUBLIME AND RIDICULOUS COLLIDE AT LONDON'S EXCLUSIVE HURLINGHAM CLUB,

WHERE REVELERS DRIVE "DODGEMS" AFTER VIEWING ANTIQUE BENTLEYS AND OTHER REVERED MODELS AT THE LOUIS VUITTON CLASSIC CAR SHOW.

GIDDY AS A REBORN SCROOGE, LONDON THRIVES AS A LEADER IN GLOBAL FINANCE, CULTURE, AND EVEN (GASP) CUISINE.

The last time London occupied center stage in world history was the "swinging sixties," when its music and fashion defined the look and sound of a generation. London is calling again. Its theater and music scenes are world leaders; its restored historic buildings and monuments glitter with gold leaf; its immaculate parks look better than ever. Most startling are the changes among its people. The millennium ended in Indonesia and the Balkans with ethnic cleansing and racial hatred. Londoners are moving in the opposite direction, making their city the world's greatest cosmopolis.

> The last time London took center stage in world history was the "swinging sixties."

For John Shepherd, a cabbie who has been threading his way through London's streets for the past 30 years, keeping pace with all this is no small task. "To do the Knowledge now is taking up to three years," he said, recalling the exam that London cab drivers have to take before they can get their license, as we swept over Waterloo Bridge on our way to Peckham in south London, where he was born. "I left school at 15 and started work in the old Covent Garden flower market." A short, well-built man with a domed, balding head, blue-gray eyes, a close mustache, and a razor-sharp wit, John is one of those archetypal Londoners who seem to have stepped straight out of *Mary Poppins* or *EastEnders*.

Adapted from "London on a Roll" by Simon Worrall: National Geographic Magazine, June 2000.

"An old cabbie once said to me, 'John, my son, if you learn one thing a day while you're doing this job, by the end of your life'"—he paused meaningfully as a gray plaque marking the onetime home of Charlie Chaplin flashed by—"'your 'ead will be full of rubbish.'"

We pulled up outside a two-story house on Elmington Road. "See the different colored brick?" said John, pointing up at the wall. "That's where it was hit with a German bomb." From Brunswick Park, along the street, we could hear the sound of children playing. "I did the Knowledge in the afternoons while working at the flower market. In those days you had what was called the Blue Book, which had all the different runs in it. You would get a map, and you would study the route, with all the backstreets, and write them down. Then you would go out on your bike and follow the route. The hardest to remember were all the little alleyways and backstreets. We used to call them 'rat runs.'" He paused. "You can't use most of them now. They're closing them off."

Not closing, exactly; "calming" is the official term. The addition of speed bumps to London's side streets and alleys, many of which date back to medieval times, is one response to growth and traffic congestion. After decades of flight to the suburbs, London's population is expected to rise to 7.7 million during the next 20 years, approaching what it was at the start of World War II. "You've heard of road rage," said John. "Well, there's a lot of that now."

More than London's shifting topography, it is the shifts in the human landscape that bewilder Shepherd. "I feel like a dinosaur sometimes, as though they're just waiting for people like me to die out," he said, as we settled on a bench in Brunswick Park. As a child he had played a game called Knock Down Ginger in the streets and watched barrage balloons floating overhead to ward off the Luftwaffe's planes. Today kids play video games, and the Germans are allies. Gone too is the almost exclusively white community into which he

> I don't see them as colored people. They're just my mates.

was born. The boys playing soccer in front of us were mostly of Pakistani or West Indian descent. When I asked John what he thought of mixed marriages, he paused and said with a wink, "A robin won't mate with a blackbird, will it?"

Daniel Shepherd, John's 21-year-old son, resembles John. He has the same slightly slanting, blue-gray eyes, prominent ears, and round face. But his attitudes couldn't be more different. "If I talk to someone, race is not the first thing I notice," he told me during his lunch break at Dorling Kindersley, the publisher, where he was doing a student internship. By coincidence his office is in Covent Garden, a few yards from where his father once worked and met Daniel's mother. "I have loads of friends who are black. I have got a lot of Indian friends at work. I don't see them as colored people. They're just my mates."

The whole world lives in London. Walk down Oxford Street and you will see Indians and Colombians, Bangladeshis and Ethiopians, Pakistanis and Russians, Melanesians and Malaysians. Fifty nationalities with communities of more than 5,000 make their home in the city, and on any given day 300 languages are spoken. It is estimated that by 2010 the population will be almost 30 percent ethnic minorities, the majority born in the U.K. Most of these Londoners are the children and in some cases the grandchildren of the many thousands who came here from the Caribbean and the Indian subcontinent during the 50s and 60s, after the British Empire imploded.

Annas Ali, a 17-year-old Londoner of Bangladeshi descent, feels deeply rooted in British society. "I have been here all my life," he told me, as we dodged our way through the festive crowds filling Brick Lane in the East End for Baishakhi Mela, the Bangladeshi New Year. The neighborhood is known as Bangla Town. Union Jacks fluttered next to the green-and-red flag of Bangladesh. Indian music echoed off Victorian brick houses. "I was born at Mile End hospital a half mile away and grew

Embracing the moment, Neil Williams and Joanne Evans enjoy a summer Sunday. "Mixed relationships are more accepted here than in the U.S.," says Evans.

up in Hunton Street. My father had a restaurant there."

Annas Ali himself is eclectic. With his dark skin, raven black hair, and lustrous brown eyes, he reminded me of Mowgli in the *Jungle Book*. But his hair was cut in the latest London style: short in back, long and slicked back with gel at the front. He is a devout Muslim, an Asian Londoner who talks Cockney English. The gold rings on his fingers were from India, his stylish, midnight blue cardigan—"pure wool," he told me proudly—from Prohibito, a clothes shop on Oxford Street popular among teenagers. "I want to go into fashion," he said. "I want to go to the London School of Fashion."

Two weeks before I met Annas, a nail bomb went off in Brick Lane—one of three that shook the city last year. The newspapers ran features about neo-Nazi groups with names like Combat 18 and speculated about a coming racial war. But the bombings last year were not part of a broader trend. They were a desperate attempt by a single individual pathologically at odds with his times to stop the racial mixing that, with a typically British lack of hype, has been going on for a generation.

"It's the holy grail of all societies to have the energy that hybridity brings without the distressing divisions," Trevor Phillips told me as we sat in the living room of his house in

continued on page 318

Pinstripes and polish mark Leadenhall Market in the City, London's square-mile financial district and the world's largest hub of international banking. "City men can afford the luxury of a shine," says Kathryn Ford.

40

continued from page 315

Stanmore, a leafy suburb on the northern fringes of the city. Born in London of Guyanese origins, Phillips is one of Britain's best known broadcasters and the chairman of the London Arts Board. "We're just reaching for it here. We're just on the edge of being able to do it."

Outside, a Volvo dozed in the driveway. Through a sliding glass door I could see a well-mowed lawn. It was every middle-class Englishman's idea of suburban comfort. What struck me even more was this black Londoner's ease in discussing a subject that in the United States can be fissile material.

"In America you always have to choose: I'm black, or I'm not black," he said. "When I go to New York to visit my sisters, I can, if I so choose, never speak to someone who is not black. Here that is not possible. There are so many different Londons that jostle side by side, and so many different kinds of people who live here, and we have a whole set of manners and ways of looking at people who are different from us that allow us to live right next door to them. To be cool about it."

It is this convivial mixing of the races, not just its diversity, that is so special about London. "There is a great amount of intermarrying here," says Sunand Prasad, an architect of Indian origin whose family emigrated to London 30 years ago. "The races used to be quite distinct, but rather than the edges becoming ever more sharply defined, as they are in France or the States, they are really beginning to blur."

Along with its cosmopolitanism and tolerance, London's surging economy is drawing a new wave of migrants—not from the Caribbean or Africa but from across the Channel. "London is very attractive to French people at the moment," said Christophe Beauvilain, a 32-year-old executive at Goldman Sachs, as we rushed across the fields of Picardy on Eurostar,

> It's the holy grail of all societies to have that energy that hybridity brings without the distressing divisions.

the high-speed rail link between Paris and London. It was Sunday night, and the train was packed with French returning to London after a weekend at home. "It is much more dynamic in terms of fashion or night life. And it's more entrepreneurial. All the headquarters of the big financial institutions are here. You make more money. The taxes are lower."

Since the 16th century London's financial district, known as the City or the Square Mile, has been one of the most powerful business centers in the world. Today, with 539 foreign banks, it is the most international: More than 437 billion dollars flows through its foreign currency markets every day, far more than anywhere else in the world. The value of London's economy—$162 billion—is larger than that of many countries, including Poland, Singapore, and even Switzerland.

Geographically and politically the United Kingdom may be on the fringes of Europe, but London has become, economically and culturally, the de facto capital of Europe. At the same time, it feels more European than ever. This can be seen in the way Londoners have discovered the street. When I was young, Soho was a backwater stalked by sleazy men in raincoats, but as I walked around late on a warm summer evening, there was a boisterous, carnival atmosphere. People spilled out of pubs with their pints; a young couple stood locked in a passionate embrace in an alleyway off Dean Street; gangs of girls with bare stomachs and studs in their navels sat at pavement cafés gossiping or ogling the boys.

"My picture of London before I came here was very old-fashioned—people drinking tea at 4 P.M. and everyone being very polite," said Ximena Cordova, a 24-year-old from Bolivia. With her Latin looks and azure blue sweater, set off by a white lily tucked into her hair, Ximena looked like one of those brilliant, exotic creatures you find in the rain forest. "But London is a very free place. I lived in Barcelona before, and London is much more tolerant, much more cosmopolitan."

London's broad-mindedness has made the city a magnet for homosexuals. "I feel like I'm part of the driving force of London," said Carl Gobey, 23, who is gay. A sociology student from Britain's second city, Birmingham, he is one of the 30,000 young people from other parts of Britain who pack a suitcase and, with a bit of money and a lot of hope, head for London each year to reinvent themselves. "Everything is here—different nationalities, different people, different styles and fashions. Anything you want to be, any life you want to lead: You can find it."

This golden age has a dark side. In a church graveyard in Brixton, I saw marijuana and other drugs being dealt among the tombstones. Across the road at the Fridge, 2,000 Generation Xers were dancing to the sound of Basement Jaxx, one of the hottest acts on the city's club scene. Many of the revelers were clearly high. A whole cottage industry of illegal drug factories supplies "dance drugs," such as ecstasy, amphetamines, and the anesthetic GHB. Hard drugs are also increasingly available. Last year some of London's poorest areas were flooded with three-dollar bags of heroin. "It's easier to get drugs in London than it is to get a taxi," John Ellis, a 24-year-old recovering addict, told me.

At last it is also just as easy to get good food. A journey to London used to be a gastronomic Calvary, but with more than 6,000 restaurants serving dishes from every corner of the planet, London may now be the most cosmopolitan culinary center anywhere in the world.

"The sea bass is the top bollocks today," said Steve Carter, the Yorkshire-born head chef at Bank, a huge—and hugely popular—new restaurant in the heart of the West End. I had signed up to be a sous-chef for a day, and now I was struggling into a black chef's jacket, a pair of black-and-white pinstripe cotton trousers, and an apron. It was nearly midday, and the lunchtime rush was building. My fellow souschefs were from Sweden, New Zealand, Australia, France, and Italy. Steve strode up and down like Nelson before a naval battle, tasting sauces, checking ingredients. "I'm a bit worried about the langoustine," he said. "I have only a hundred portions. Let's just hope it's enough."

Bank is owned by Tony Allan, a working-class Londoner who took one of the city's oldest trades, fishmongering, and remade it. The fish served at his restaurants comes from sustainable sources, he says. Genetically modified food is prohibited—notices at each restaurant read, "This is a GM-free zone!"

"I was a chef originally," Tony explained, as Bank began to fill up. With his glowing tan, white jeans, denim shirt, and flowing locks, he looked like a pop star. "But I got the sack because I was always complaining about the quality of the fish. So I started going to the coastal markets, places like Hastings on the south coast, buying fish to supply to restaurants. One man with a van sort of thing."

Fourteen years later he supplies three-quarters of all fish used by London's restaurants, the van is a Ferrari, and Bank Group Restaurants is a publicly traded company worth 100 million pounds (160 million dollars). Such success stories have a long tradition; London's most famous bit of folklore tells of a poor country boy named Dick Whittington, who arrives with his possessions tied in a bundle at the end of a stick and ends up rich and famous. And though Allan isn't the mayor of London, as Whittington was, it is entrepreneurs like him—savvy, ambitious, quick to spot the main chance—who have always made London rich. Today he lives in a mansion in Kent and indulges his passion for falconry.

Like many of London's new restaurants, Bank has its kitchen in the middle of the dining area—a stage on which, twice daily, a noisy, olfactory drama is performed. Theater and spectacle have always been at the heart of London's life. Or, as Shakespeare put it: All the world's a stage. At Bank, the clank of pots and the billowing of smoke were the stage effects; my fellow sous-chefs and I, the actors. For maximum theatrical effect we bellowed each order at the top of our lungs and sprinkled our dialogue with French.

"105!" roared Steve Carter, spiking an order. "One chateaubriand! One calf's liver!"

"*Ca marche!*" came the answering cry from inside the kitchen.

My job was to see that each dish was accompanied by the correct side orders. By 1:20 P.M.

> **L**ondon has become, economically and culturally, the de facto capital of Europe.

we were handling 55 main courses simultaneously, and I was sweating like a stevedore.

Through the plate-glass windows I could see the crowds surging along the sidewalks. Black cabs weaved through the cars and buses on their way to Trafalgar Square. As I watched them go by, I felt a wave of affection for this great city, which, like an ancient coral reef, has gone on shifting and growing, adapting itself to the needs and the dreams of each new generation for nearly 2,000 years.

Critical Responses

1. What is the focus of the text of this article? What is the focus of the photographs? How does each relate to the other—or not—and what are the implications?

2. What do the rigors of becoming a cabbie in London suggest about the city's values? What does the term for the course of study, "The Knowledge," itself imply?

3. How is London a "melting pot"? How, in this regard, does it compare to a major metropolitan U.S. city?

4. What, on the other hand, are some ways in which Londoners are divided? Are these unique to London? Or are they typical in modern cities?

Writing Topics

1. Though related, concepts such as "diversity" and "integration" are not quite the same. Defining each, and distinguishing between them, discuss ways in which London exemplifies the one and the other.

2. Taking this idea in a somewhat different direction, consider what "multiculturalism" means objectively as well as the values implied by the term. How does multiculturalism contribute to the overall culture of a specific place—whether it be a college campus or a city? Can it detract in any way?

3. Compare this depiction of London with that of New York in Joel Swerdlow's "Tale of Three Cities." What makes each a cosmopolitan city? How does each contribute to and expand your idea of what a cosmopolitan city is or could be?

4. How, according to Worrall, would Londoners view the couple embracing in Cobb's photograph? Do you agree that an American would have a different perspective? What about the observations about race and identity in London versus America? Does your experience bear them out, at least on the American side?

Further Explorations

1. Write a descriptive essay about a place you know well—whether it be a home town, a neighborhood, or a city—focusing on its demographic features. Does the demographic profile make it an attractive place? How and why, and, crucially, to whom?

2. What was London like in the 1960s? Research the question, whether individually or in groups. How do your findings illuminate points made in this article? How do they illuminate the character of the 60s in general? Are the themes of the period familiar to you? Or do they seem remote, in place and time?

Comstock/Jupiter Images

> Go confidently in the direction of your dreams.
>
> **Henry David Thoreau**

Communication and Personal Identity

Kate is a 35-year-old physician's assistant. She is also a mother, an aunt, and a sister. Earlier in her life, Kate was a teenager, a student, and a fierce soccer player. One day, she may be retired and a grandmother. Like Kate, your identity changes over time. When you were 5 or 6, you probably defined yourself as your parents' son or daughter. In doing so, you implicitly recognized sex, race, and social class as parts of your identity. In high school, you may have described yourself in terms of academic abilities ("I'm better at math than at history"), athletic roles ("I'm a guard"), leadership positions ("I'm president of the Drama Club"), your social circle ("I hang out with Cindy and Mike"), or future plans ("I'm going to study hospital administration when I go to college").

If you entered college shortly after completing high school, you're probably

MindTap

Review the chapter **Learning Objectives** and **Start** with a quick warm up activity.

SHARPEN YOUR SKILL

At the end of this chapter, refer to the Sharpen Your Skill features, Reflecting on Your Identity Scripts and Your Looking-Glass Self, to apply concepts from Chapter 3.

thinking of yourself in terms of a major, a career path, and perhaps a relationship you hope will span the years ahead. If you worked or committed to a relationship before starting or returning to college, you may already have a sense of yourself as a professional and a family member. By now, you've probably made some decisions about your spiritual beliefs and your political and social values.

As you think about the different ways you've defined yourself over the years, you'll realize that the self is not fixed firmly at one time and constant thereafter. Instead, the self is a process that evolves and changes throughout our lives. Communication with others is one of the greatest influences on our personal identities. In this chapter, we explore how the self develops continually through communication with others.

WHAT IS THE SELF?

Read, highlight and take notes online.

The **self** is a process of internalizing and acting from social perspectives that we learn in the process of communication. At first, this may seem like a complicated way to define the self. As we will see, however, this definition directs our attention to some important insights into what is complicated: the human self.

The Self Arises in Communication With Others

The most basic insight into the self is that it isn't something we are born with. Instead, the self develops only as we communicate with others and participate in the social world. From the moment we are born, we interact with others. We learn how they see us, and we internalize many of their views of who we are and should be.

Communication With Family Members   For most of us, family members are the first important influence on how we see ourselves (Bergen & Braithwaite, 2009). Parents and other family members communicate who we are and what we are worth through *direct definition*, *identity scripts*, and *attachment styles*.

Direct definition, as the term implies, is communication that explicitly tells us who we are by labeling us and our behaviors. For instance, parents might say, "You're my little girl" or "You're a big boy" and thus communicate to the child what sex he or she is. Having been labeled *boy* or *girl*, the child then pays attention to how others talk about boys and girls to figure out what it means to be a certain sex. Parents' own gender stereotypes typically are communicated to children, so daughters may also be told, "Be nice to your friends" and "Don't mess up your clothes." Sons, on the other hand, are more likely to be told, "Stick up for yourself" and "Don't cry." As we hear these messages, we pick up our parents' and society's gender expectations. Direct definition also takes place as family members respond to children's behaviors. If a child is praised for dusting furniture, being helpful is reinforced as part of the child's self-concept. Positive labels enhance our self-esteem: "You are smart," "You're sweet," "You're great at baseball." Negative labels can damage children's self-esteem: "You're a troublemaker," "You're stupid," and "You're impossible" are messages that can demolish a child's sense of self-worth.

Identity scripts are another way family members communicate who we are and should be. Psychologists define identity scripts as rules for how we are supposed to live and who we are supposed to be (Berne, 1964; Harris, 1969). Like the scripts for plays, identity scripts define our roles, how we are to play them, and basic elements in the plot we are supposed to have for our lives. Think back to your childhood to identify some of the principal scripts that operated in your family. Did you learn, "Always be prepared for emergencies," "We give back to our community," or "Live by God's word"? These are examples of identity scripts families teach us.

Rob Gage/Taxi/Getty Images

Family members' communication shapes personal identity.

Children seldom author, or even edit, initial identity scripts. In fact, children are generally not even conscious of learning identity scripts. As adults, however, we are no longer passive tablets on which others can define who we are. We have the capacity to review the identity scripts that were given to us and to challenge and change those that do not fit who we now choose to be.

Finally, parents communicate who we are through **attachment styles**, which are patterns of parenting that teach us who we and others are and how to relate to others. From extensive studies of interaction between parents and children, John Bowlby (1973, 1988) developed the theory that most of us learn attachment styles in our relationship with our first care givers—usually with parents. They communicate how they see us, others, and relationships. In turn, we are likely to internalize their views as our own. The first relationship is especially important because it shapes expectations for later relationships (Rhodewalt, 2007). Four distinct attachment styles have been identified (Figure 3.1).

A child is most likely to develop a *secure attachment style* when the primary caregiver interacts in a consistently attentive and loving way with the child. In response, the child develops a positive sense of self-worth ("I am lovable") and a positive view of others ("People are loving and can be trusted"). People with secure attachment styles tend to be outgoing, affectionate, and able to handle the normal challenges and disappointments of close relationships without losing self-esteem. Securely attached individuals tend to have more secure relationships (Rowe & Carnelley, 2005) than less securely attached individuals.

A child may develop a *fearful attachment style* if the primary caregiver communicates in negative, rejecting, or abusive ways to the child.

Parents' communication is a major influence on identity.

Children who are treated unkindly often infer that they are unworthy of love and that others are not loving. Thus, they learn to see themselves as unlovable and others as rejecting. Although they may want close bonds with others, they fear that others will not love them and that they themselves are not lovable.

A caregiver who is disinterested, rejecting, or abusive may also lead a child to develop a *dismissive attachment style*, which makes the child tend to dismiss others as unworthy. People with dismissive attachment styles have a positive view of themselves and a low regard for others and relationships. This may lead them to regard relationships as unnecessary and undesirable.

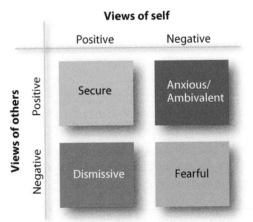

FIGURE 3.1
Styles of Attachment

> **AMELIA** *When I was in high school, I babysat to make money. One little girl I watched was very stand offish. No matter how hard I tried to play with Liza and be friends, she kept her distance. But sometimes I would see her looking at me almost longingly like she wanted to play with me. When her parents were around, they were focused on work or each other. If Liza needed something or spoke up, they acted as if she was interrupting them.*

Last is the *anxious/ambivalent attachment style,* which is the most complex of the four. Each of the other three styles results from a consistent pattern of treatment by a caregiver. However, the anxious/ambivalent style is fostered by *inconsistent* treatment from the caregiver. Sometimes the adult is loving and attentive, at other times indifferent or rejecting. The caregiver's communication is not only inconsistent but also unpredictable. He or she may respond positively to something a child does on Monday and react negatively to the same behavior on Tuesday. Naturally, this unpredictability creates anxiety in a child. Because children tend to assume that adults are right, they often believe they themselves are the source of any problem—that they are unlovable or deserve others' abuse. People who have high anxiety about attachments are likely to avoid or minimize attachments (Brenning, Soenens, Braet, & Bosmans, 2011).

In adult life, people who have anxious/ambivalent attachment styles know that others can be loving and affirming, but they also know that others can hurt them and be unloving. Reflecting the pattern displayed by the caregiver, people with anxious/ambivalent attachment styles often are inconsistent themselves. One day they invite affection; the next day they deny needing closeness. An interesting study by Tim Cole and Laura Leets (1999) found that people with anxious/ambivalent attachment styles often form relationships with television characters. It may feel safer to be in relationships with television characters than with real people.

Unless we consciously work to change the attachment styles we learned in our first close relationships, they tend to affect how we communicate in our adult relationships (Bornstein & Languirand, 2003; Bowlby, 1988; Guerrero, 1996). However, we can modify our attachment styles by challenging unconstructive views of us communicated in our early years and by forming relationships that foster secure connections today (Banse, 2004). To learn more about attachment theory, use MindTap for *Communication in Our Lives* to access **WebLink 3.1**.

MindTap™

Communication With Peers A second major influence on our self-concepts is communication with peers. From childhood playmates to work associates, friends, and romantic partners, we interact with peers throughout our lives. As we do, we gain further direct definitions that tell us how others see us. In turn, this affects how we see ourselves. As we interact with peers, we engage in **social comparison,** which involves comparing ourselves with others to gauge our talents, attractiveness, abilities, skills, and so forth (Stapel &

We measure our abilities against those of peers.

Edwin Verin/Shutterstock.com

Blanton, 2006). We measure ourselves in relation to others in two ways. First, we compare ourselves with others to decide whether we are like them or different from them. Are we the same age, color, or religion? Do we have similar backgrounds and social and political beliefs?

Peers are particularly strong in commenting directly on conformity to expectations of gender. Some college-age men think drinking and sexual activity embody masculinity. Men who are not interested in drinking and hooking up may be ridiculed and excluded for not being "real men" (Cross, 2008; Kimmel, 2008). Women who don't wear popular brands of clothing or who weigh more than what is considered ideal may be belittled and excluded for being unfeminine (Adler, 2007; Barash, 2006).

Assessing similarity and difference allows us to decide with whom we fit. Research has shown that people generally are most comfortable with others who are like them, so we tend to gravitate toward those we regard as similar (Amodio & Showers, 2006; Chen, Luo, Yue, Xu, & Zhaoyang, 2009; Lutz-Zois, Bradley, Mihalik, & Moorman-Eavers, 2006). However, interacting only with people like us can impoverish our understandings of ourselves and the world.

We also use social comparison to measure ourselves in relation to others. Am I as good a goalie as Jenny? Am I as smart as Sam? We continuously refine our self-image by comparing ourselves to others on various criteria of judgment. This is normal and necessary if we are to develop realistic self-concepts. However, we should be wary of what psychologists call upward comparison, which is the tendency to compare ourselves to people who exceed us in what they have or can do (Tugend, 2011). For most of us, it isn't constructive to judge our attractiveness in relation to that of movie stars and models or our athletic ability in relation to that of professional athletes.

KEVIN *I learned more about myself and about being white when I was assigned to room with a black guy my freshman year. I'd never interacted much with blacks, and I'd never had a black friend, but I got really close with my roommate. Carl helped me see a lot of things I take for granted that he can't because of his skin. For example, people assume I'm here because I earned a good record in high school, but a lot of people think Carl got in just because he's black and the college had to meet its minority quota. His SAT was higher than mine and so are his grades, but people believe I'm smart and he's a quota admission.*

Communication With Society   A third influence on our self-concepts is interaction with society in general. As we observe and interact with others and media and as we participate in institutions, we learn how society regards each sex, race, sexual orientation, and socioeconomic class. We also learn broad cultural values.

Western society encourages people to perceive themselves as individuals and to form separate families in adulthood. In contrast, traditional Indian culture emphasizes collective identity, and households under the same roof often include grandparents, aunts, uncles, and cousins (Lustig & Koester, 1999). Western society also encourages competition, whereas many Asian societies teach children to place emphasis on cooperation and teamwork (Yum, 2000).

Media is a primary agent in teaching social perspectives. When we read popular magazines, watch films, and visit sites on the Web, we are inundated with messages about how women and men are supposed to look and act, who has status, and so forth. Media shape teens' views of sex and sexuality—what is appropriate and "cool" (Bodey & Wood, 2009; Wood, 2010).

HEALTH COMMUNICATION

Self-Help: A Healthier Self?

Do you love too much, too little, or the wrong people? Are you guilty of negative thinking? If so, there's a self-help book—or a dozen—for you. Don't want a book? No problem, buy self-help video and audio products, attend seminars, or hire a personal coach. You can join a support group with 12 steps or 7 principles. It's all part of the multibillion dollar self-help industry. And don't forget television programs such as *The* Swan (aired 2004), Extreme *Makeover* (aired 2002–2006) and *The Biggest Loser* (is being aired 2004–present), which also tell us to take charge of fixing ourselves with self-discipline perhaps along with multiple surgeries.

Although the self-help industry is wildly popular today, it's not exactly new. The first self-help book was published in 1859 by Samuel Smiles. Titled *Self-Help* and appropriately self-published, Smiles' book opened by telling readers "Heaven helps those who help themselves." Within a year of publication, the book sold 20,000 copies, extraordinary for that era. Another early self-help author was Dale Carnegie. After a short stint as a salesman, Carnegie failed as an actor and wound up broke, unemployed and living at the YMCA in New York. That's where he started teaching a public speaking course that formed the basis of *How to Win Friends and Influence People* (1936), which was a self-help manual for millions of readers.

Despite the popularity of self-help, caution may be wise. Steve Salerno, former editor of *Men's Health* magazine's books program, doesn't think much of self-help books. In *SHAM* (2005), a critique of the self-help industry, he writes that "self-help is an enterprise wherein people holding the thinnest of credentials diagnose in basically normal people symptoms of inflated or invented maladies, so that they may then implement remedies that have never been shown to work" (p. 1).

The institutions that organize our society further communicate social perspectives by the values they uphold. For example, our judicial system reminds us that as a society we value laws and punish those who break them. The number of schools and the levels of education in America inform us that our society values learning. At the same time, institutions reflect prevailing social prejudices. For instance, we may be a lawful society, but wealthy defendants often can buy better "justice" than poor ones. Similarly, although we claim to offer equal educational opportunities to all, students whose families have money and influence often can get into better schools than students whose families have fewer resources. These and other values are so thoroughly woven into the fabric of our culture that we learn them with little effort or awareness.

The Self-Fulfilling Prophecy   One particularly powerful way in which communication shapes the self is the self-fulfilling prophecy, which we discussed in Chapter 2. Self-fulfilling prophecies operate when we act in ways that bring about expectations or judgments of ourselves. If you have done poorly in classes in which teachers didn't seem to respect you and have done well with teachers who thought you were smart, then you know what a self-fulfilling prophecy is. The prophecies that we act to fulfill usually are first communicated to us by others' direct definitions, identity scripts, and attachment styles. Because we often internalize others' perspectives, we may label ourselves as they do and then act to fulfill our own labels.

TERRY   *I can really identify with the self-fulfilling prophecy idea. In the second grade, my family moved from our farm to a city where my dad could find work. The first week of class in my new school, we had show and tell. When it was my turn, as soon as I started talking the other kids started laughing at me. I had been raised on a farm in the rural South, and the other kids were from the city. They thought I talked funny, and they made fun of my accent—called me "hillbilly" and "redneck." From then on, I avoided public speaking like the plague. I thought I couldn't speak to others. Last year, I finally took a course in public speaking, and I made a B. It took me a long time to challenge the label that I was a bad public speaker.*

Many of us believe things about ourselves that are inaccurate. Sometimes labels that were once true aren't any longer, but we continue to believe them and act to fulfill them. In other cases, the labels were never valid, but we may believe them anyway. Unfortunately, children often are labeled "slow" or "stupid" when the real problem is that they have physiological difficulties such as impaired vision or hearing. Even when the true source of difficulty is discovered, the children may have already internalized a destructive self-fulfilling prophecy.

The Self Is Multidimensional

Although we use the word *self* as if it referred to a single entity, in reality the self has many dimensions. You have a physical self that includes your size, shape, skin, hair and eye colors, and so forth. In addition, you have a cognitive self that includes your intelligence, aptitudes, and education. You have an emotional self-concept. Are you interpersonally sensitive? Do you have a hot temper? Are you generally optimistic or pessimistic? You have a social self. Some people are extraverted, whereas others are more reserved. Our social selves also include our roles: daughter or son, student, worker, parent, volunteer, partner in a committed relationship. Each of us also has a moral self that is composed of ethical and spiritual principles we believe in and try to follow. As Carlyle points out, the different dimensions of ourselves sometimes seem at odds with one another.

CARLYLE *On my own, like with friends or family, I'm pretty quiet—even shy, you could say. But my job requires me to be real outgoing and sociable. I tend bar, and people expect me to kid around and talk with them and stuff. Believe me, if I were as quiet with my customers as I am with my friends, my tips would drop to nothing. It's like when I'm in my work role, I'm Mr. Hail-fellow-well-met, but away from work I'm pretty reserved.*

The Self Is a Process

The self develops over time; it is a process. A baby perceives no boundaries between its body and a nipple, a hand that tickles, or a breeze. As an infant has experiences and as others respond to him or her, the child gradually begins to develop **ego boundaries**, which define where the self stops and the rest of the world begins. This is the beginning of a self-concept: the realization that one is a separate entity.

As infants begin to differentiate themselves from the rest of the world, the self starts to develop. Infants and young children listen to and observe others to define themselves and to become competent in the identities others assign to them (Kohlberg, 1958; Piaget, 1932/1965). For instance, children work to figure out what it takes to be nice, tough, and responsible, and they strive to become competent at embodying those qualities. The ways we define ourselves vary as we mature. Struggling to be a good mud-cake maker at age 4 gives way to striving for popularity in high school and to succeeding in professional and family roles later in life.

Of course, we all enter the world with certain abilities and limits, which constrain the possibilities of who we can be. Someone without the genes to be tall and coordinated, for instance, probably is not going to be a star forward in basketball. Beyond genetic limits, however, we have considerable freedom to create who we will be.

We Internalize and Act From Social Perspectives

We've already noted that in developing a self, we internalize many of the perspectives of others. Let's now look more closely at how we internalize both the perspectives of individuals who are significant in our lives and the general perspective of our society.

Particular Others We first encounter the perspectives of **particular others**. As the term implies, these are the viewpoints of specific people who are significant to us. Mothers, fathers, siblings, and often day-care providers are particular others who are significant to most infants. In addition, we may be very close to aunts, uncles, grandparents, godparents, and others. Children who grow up in large, extended families often have a great many particular others who affect how they come to see themselves.

> **SHENNOA** *My grandmother was the biggest influence on me. I lived with her while my mama worked, and she taught me to take myself seriously. She's the one who told me I should go to college and plan a career so that I wouldn't have to depend on somebody else. She's the one who told me to stand up for myself and not let others tell me what to do or believe in. But she did more than just tell me to be a strong person. That's how she was, and I learned just by watching her. A lot of who I am is modeled on my grandmother.*

The process of seeing ourselves through others' eyes is called **reflected appraisal**. It means that we see ourselves in terms of the appraisals reflected in others' eyes. The process has also been called the "looking-glass self" because others are mirrors who reflect who we are (Cooley, 1912). Reflected appraisals are not confined to childhood but continue throughout our lives. When a teacher communicates that a student is smart, the student may come to see himself or herself that way. In professional life, coworkers and supervisors reflect their appraisals of us when they communicate that we're on the fast track, average, or unsuited to our position. The appraisals that others communicate shape how we see ourselves. In turn, how we see ourselves affects how we communicate. Thus, if you see yourself as an interesting conversationalist, you're likely to communicate that confidence when you talk with others.

Leigh M. Wilco

We see ourselves in the looking glass of others' eyes.

The Generalized Other   The second social perspective that influences how we see ourselves is called the **perspective of the generalized other**. The generalized other is the collection of rules, roles, and attitudes endorsed by the specific culture in which we live (Mead, 1934). Modern Western culture emphasizes gender, race, sexual orientation, and economic class as central to personal identity (Andersen & Collins, 2006; Wood, 1995b, 2005). Each of these social groupings represents a standpoint, which we discussed in Chapter 2.

North American culture views race as a primary aspect of personal identity (González, Houston, & Chen, 2012). The white race historically has been privileged in the United States. In the early years of this country, it was considered normal and right for white men to own black women, men, and children and to require them to work for no wages and in poor conditions. Later, it was considered natural that white men could vote but black men could not. Clearly, racial prejudice has diminished substantially. Even so, the upper levels of government, education, and business are dominated by white men, whereas people of color continue to fight overt and covert discrimination in many spheres of society.

WEN-SHU   *My family moved here when I was 9 years old. Because I look Asian, people make assumptions about me. They assume I am quiet (true), I am good at math (not true), and I defer to men and elders (true with regard to elders but not men). People also see all Asians as the same, but Taiwanese are as different from mainland Chinese as French Caucasians are from U.S. Caucasians. The first thing people notice about me is my race, and they make too many assumptions about what it means.*

Gender, another important facet of identity in Western culture, also is communicated through social practices and institutions (Martin & Finn, 2010). Historically, men—specifically, white men—have been seen as more

valuable than women and more entitled to privileges. In the 1800s, women weren't allowed to own property, attend college, or vote. Although there has been great progress in achieving equality between the sexes, in some respects women and men still are not considered equal or treated as such (Kaufman & Kimmel, 2011).

Western cultures have strong gender prescriptions. Girls and women are expected to be caring and cooperative, whereas boys and men are supposed to be independent and competitive. Consequently, women who are competitive and men who are gentle may receive social disapproval for violating gender prescriptions. Gender prescriptions also specify ideal body images—tall and muscular for men; slender or thin and not too tall for women.

A third aspect of identity that cultural communication establishes as salient is sexual orientation. Western culture's view that heterosexuality is normal and right is communicated not only directly but also through privileges given to heterosexuals but denied to gay men, lesbians, bisexuals, trans and gender non-conforming people. For example, a woman and man who love each other can be married, and their commitment can be recognized religiously and legally. Two men or two women who love each other are not allowed to marry in most states, although domestic partnerships are increasingly recognized. Heterosexual spouses can obtain insurance coverage for their partners and can will them money tax free, but people with other sexual orientations often cannot. By 2010, nearly 300 colleges had added gender identity and expression to their nondiscrimination policies, many have designated some bathrooms as available to everyone, and many have passed gender-neutral housing policies so that transgender students are not forced to live with people with whom they don't identify (Tilsley, 2010). Although biases against sexual orientation and gender identity are decreasing, they still very much affect how we are viewed and treated.

SANDI *I've known I was lesbian since I was in high school, but only in the last year have I come out to others. As soon as I tell someone I'm lesbian, they see me differently. Even people who have known me a long time act like I've developed spots or something. Some of my girlfriends don't want to hug or touch me anymore, like they think I'm suddenly going to come on to them. Guys act as if I'm from another planet. It's really strange that sexual orientation makes so much difference in how others see you. I mean, relative to other things like character, personality, and intelligence, who you sleep with is pretty unimportant.*

A fourth dimension of identity, socioeconomic class, is also central to the generalized other's perspective in Western culture. Socioeconomic class isn't just the amount of money a person has. It's a basic part of how we understand our place in the world and how we think, feel, and act (Lawless, 2012). Socioeconomic class affects everything from the careers we pursue to the schools and lifestyles we see as possibilities for ourselves. Members of the middle and upper classes assume that they will attend college and enter good professions, whereas people from the working class may be directed toward vocational training regardless of their academic achievements. In such patterns, we see how the perspective of the generalized other shapes our identities and our concrete lives.

ROCHELLE *I got so mad in high school. I had a solid A average, and ever since I was 12 I had planned to go to college. But when the guidance counselor talked with me at the start of my senior year, she encouraged me to apply to a technical school that is near my home. When I said I thought my grades should get me into a good college, she did this double-take, like, "Your kind doesn't go to college." My parents both work in a mill and so do all my relatives, but does that mean that I can't have a different future? What really burned me was that a lot of girls who had average grades but came from "the right families" were told to apply to colleges.*

It's important to realize that social perspectives on race, sex, sexual orientation, and socioeconomic class interact. Race intersects gender, so women of color often experience double oppression and devaluation in our culture. Class and sexual orientation also interact: Homophobia tends to be pronounced among people in the working class, so a lesbian or gay person in a poor community may be socially ostracized. Socioeconomic class and gender are also interlinked; women are far more likely than men to live at the poverty level (Andersen & Collins, 2006; Kaufman & Kimmel, 2011). Intersections of race and class mean that minority members of the working class often are not treated as well as working-class whites (Rothenberg, 2006).

As we internalize the generalized other's perspective, we come to share many of the views and values of our society. Shared understandings are essential for collective life. If we all made up our own rules, there would be no shared standards and collective life would be chaotic. Yet, shared understandings are not carved in stone: People sometimes work to change how their society operates. Each of us has an ethical responsibility to think critically about which social views to accept and use as guides for our own behaviors, attitudes, and values. This suggests a fourth proposition about the self.

Lifesize/Getty Images

Social perspectives on same-sex relationships have changed over time.

Social Perspectives on the Self Are Constructed and Changeable

The generalized other's perspectives are not fixed. They are constructed and therefore can be changed if enough members of a society challenge them.

Constructed Social perspectives are created in particular cultures at specific times to support dominant ideologies, or the beliefs and comfort of those in power. When we reflect on social values, we realize that they are arbitrary and tend to serve the interests of those who benefit from prevailing values. The constructed nature of social values becomes especially obvious when we consider how greatly values differ between cultures and within particular cultures over time. For example, in Sweden, Denmark, and Norway, marriages between members of the same sex are given legal and social recognition.

Prescriptions for femininity and masculinity vary over time within a particular culture. In the 1700s and 1800s, women in the United States were defined as too delicate to engage in hard labor. During World Wars I and II, however, women were expected to do "men's work" while men were at war. When the men returned home, society once again decreed that women were too weak to perform labor, and they were reassigned to home and hearth.

Social prescriptions for men also have changed. The rugged he-man who was the ideal in the 1800s used his six-shooter to dispose of unsavory rustlers and relied on physical strength to farm. After the Industrial Revolution, physical strength and bravado gave way to business acumen, and money replaced muscle as a sign of manliness. As women, men, and families change, ideals of femininity and masculinity continue to evolve.

Although there is still prejudice against people who are not heterosexual, it is gradually diminishing. Laws have been enacted to protect lesbians and gays against housing and job discrimination. As social views of gender, race, class, and a range of sexualities evolve, individuals' views of others and their own self-concepts will also change.

Changeable Social perspectives are fluid. They change in response to individual and collective efforts to weave new meanings into the fabric of common life. Racial classifications in America have changed over time. In the country's earliest years, Irish immigrants were not considered white (Morning, 2011). In the 1960s, civil rights activism launched nationwide rethinking of actions and attitudes toward non-whites. The battle to recognize and respect gays and lesbians has begun to alter social perspectives. Changes in how we view sex, race, class, (dis)ability, and sexual orientation are negotiated in communication contexts ranging from one-to-one conversations to mass and social media. Each of us has an ethical responsibility to speak out against social perspectives that we perceive as wrong or harmful. By doing so, we participate in the ongoing process of refining social perspectives.

> **JANINE** *My husband and I have really worked to share equally in our marriage. When we got married 8 years ago, we both believed women and men were equal and should have equal responsibilities for the home and family and equal power in making decisions that affect the family. But it's a lot harder to actually live that ideal than to believe in it. Both of us have struggled against our socialization that says I should cook and clean and take care of the kids and he should make big decisions about our lives. I think we've done a pretty good job of creating and living an egalitarian marriage. A lot of our friends see us as models.*

ENHANCING THE SELF

So far, we've explained how the self develops in the process of communicating with others. Building on that knowledge, we'll now explore guidelines for encouraging personal growth.

Make a Strong Commitment to Improve Yourself

The first principle for enhancing who you are is to make a firm commitment to personal growth. This isn't as easy as it might sound. A firm commitment involves more than saying, "I want to listen better" or "I want to be less judgmental." Saying these sentences is simple, but actually investing the effort to change is difficult. Changing ourselves takes persistent work. We have to be willing to invest ongoing effort. In addition, we must realize at the outset that there will be setbacks, and we can't let them derail our resolve.

Changing yourself is difficult because the self resists change. If you realize in advance that you may struggle against change, you'll be prepared for the tension that accompanies personal growth. Because change is a process and the self resists change, a firm and continuing commitment to growth is essential.

Gain Knowledge as a Basis for Personal Change

Commitment alone is insufficient to spur changes in who you are. In addition, you need several types of knowledge. First, you need to understand how the self is formed. In this chapter, we've discussed the influence of particular others and the generalized other. You may not want to accept all the views and values you were taught.

Second, you need to know how to develop goals you can achieve. Vague goals for self-improvement usually lead nowhere because they don't indicate concrete steps toward change. For instance, "I want to be better at intimate communication" is a very vague objective. You can't do anything to meet such an unclear goal until you know something about the talk that enhances and impedes intimacy. Books such as this one will help you pinpoint concrete skills that facilitate healthy intimate communication. For instance, Chapter 4 will help you develop

COMMUNICATION HIGHLIGHT

Failure on the Way to Success

Who was Babe Ruth? If you know baseball history, you probably think of him as having hit 714 home runs. He did, but he also struck out 1,330 times. R. H. Macy, who founded Macy's department store, failed in his first seven efforts to start a business. Superstar Michael Jordan was cut from his high school basketball team because he wasn't good enough. Early in his career, Walt Disney was fired from a newspaper job because his editor thought he had no good or creative ideas. The Beatles penned 59 songs before they had their first hit.

Most people who succeed fail along the way; sometimes they fail many times. If Babe Ruth had let his strikeouts defeat him, he would never have been a champion batter. The same is true of most of us. Failures and defeats are inevitable. Letting them define who we are is not inevitable.

To consider what your life would be like if you were completely unafraid of failing, complete the Communication Highlight Activity for Chapter 3 via MindTap for *Communication in Our Lives*.

listening skills, and Chapter 8 will explain how communication affects personal and social relationships.

Another important source of knowledge is other people. Perhaps you recall a time when you began a new job. If you were fortunate, you found a mentor who explained the ropes to you and gave you helpful feedback. In much the same way, others can also provide feedback on your progress in the process of change. In addition, others can serve as models. If you know someone you think is particularly skillful in supporting others, observe him or her carefully to identify concrete skills that you can tailor to suit your personal style.

Set Realistic Goals

Changing ourselves is most likely when we set realistic goals. If you are shy and want to be more extraverted, it is reasonable to try to speak up more often. On the other hand, it may not be reasonable to try to be the life of every party. Realistic goals are based on realistic standards. In a culture that emphasizes perfection, it's easy to be trapped into expecting more than is possible. A better method is to establish a series of realistic incremental goals. You might focus first on improving one communication skill. When you're satisfied with your ability at that skill, you can work on another one.

With regard to our discussion of social comparison, it's also important to select reasonable measuring sticks for yourself. It isn't realistic to compare your academic work with that of a certified genius. It isn't realistic to compare your public speaking skill with that of someone who has made public presentations for years. It is reasonable to measure your public speaking ability against that

of others who have speaking experience similar to yours. Setting realistic goals and selecting appropriate standards of comparison are important in improving yourself.

> **MIKE** *For a long time, I put myself down for not doing as well academically as a lot of my friends. They put mega-hours into studying and writing papers. I can't do that because I work 30 hours a week. Now I see that it's unfair to compare myself to them. When I compare myself to students who work as much as I do, my record is pretty good.*

Self-Disclose When Appropriate

Self-disclosure is the revelation of information about ourselves that others are unlikely to discover on their own. We self-disclose when we share private information about ourselves—our hopes, fears, feelings, thoughts, and experiences. Although we don't reveal our private selves to everyone and don't do it often even with intimates, self-disclosure is an important kind of communication.

Self-disclosure has notable values. First, sharing personal feelings, thoughts, and experiences often enhances closeness between people (Hendrick & Hendrick, 1996, 2006; Samp & Palevitz, 2009; Stafford, 2009). By extension, when others understand our private selves, they may respond to us more sensitively, as unique individuals. Self-disclosing also tends to invite others to self-disclose, so we may learn more about them. Finally, self-disclosure can affect what we know about ourselves and how we feel about who we are. For example, if we reveal a weakness or an incident of which we're ashamed, and another person accepts the disclosure without judging us negatively, we may find it easier to accept ourselves. As we reveal our hopes, fears, dreams, and feelings, we get responses from others that give us new perspectives on who we are.

Self-disclosure necessarily involves risk—the risk that others will not accept private information or that they might use it against us. Appropriate self-disclosure minimizes these risks by proceeding slowly and establishing trust. It's wise to test the waters gradually before plunging into major self-disclosures. Begin by revealing information that is personal but not highly intimate or able to damage you if exploited. Before disclosing further, observe how the other person responds to your communication and what he or she does with it. You might also pay attention to whether the other person reciprocates by disclosing personal information to you.

Accept That You Are in Process

Previously in this chapter, we saw that one characteristic of the human self is that it is continually in process. This implies that you need to accept who you are now as a starting point. You don't have to like or admire everything about yourself, but it is important to accept who you are today as a basis for going forward. The self that you are results from all the interactions and experiences in your life. Only by realizing and accepting who you are now can you move ahead.

Accepting yourself as being in process also implies that you realize you can change. Because you are in process, you are always changing and growing. Don't let yourself be hindered by defeating self-fulfilling prophecies or the fallacy of thinking that you can't change. You can change if you set realistic goals, make a genuine commitment, and then work for the changes you want. Just remember that you are not fixed as you are; you are always in the process of becoming.

Create a Supportive Context for Change

Just as it is easier to swim with the tide than against it, it is easier to change our views of ourselves when we have some support for our efforts. You can do a lot to create an environment that supports your growth by choosing contexts and people who help you realize your goals. First, think about settings. If you want to lose weight, it's better to go to restaurants that serve healthful foods and offer light choices than to go to cholesterol castles. If you want to become more extraverted, go to parties, not libraries. But libraries are a better context than parties if your goal is to improve academic performance.

JAN *I never cared a lot about clothes until I joined a sorority where the labels on your clothes are a measure of your worth. The girls compete with each other to dress the best and have the newest styles. When one of the sisters wears something out of style, she gets a lot of teasing, but really it's pressure on her to measure up to the sorority image. At first, I adopted my sisters' values, and I spent more money than I could afford on clothes. For a while I even quit making contributions at church so that I could have more money for clothes. When I finally realized I was becoming somebody I didn't like, I tried to change, but my sisters made me feel bad anytime I wasn't dressed well. Finally, I moved out rather than face that pressure all the time. It just wasn't a good place for me to be myself.*

Because how others view us affects how we see ourselves, you can create a supportive context by consciously choosing to be around people who believe in you and encourage your personal growth without being dishonest about your limitations. It's also important to steer clear of people who put you down or say you can't change. In other words, people who reflect positive appraisals of us enhance our ability to improve who we are.

Others aren't the only ones whose communication affects our self-concepts. We also communicate with ourselves, and our own messages influence how we see ourselves. One of the most crippling kinds of self-talk we can engage in is **self-sabotage**—telling ourselves we are no good, we'll never learn something, there's no point in trying to change. We may be repeating others' judgments of us, or we may be inventing negative self-fulfilling prophecies. Either way, self-sabotage undermines belief in ourselves.

Distinguished therapist Albert Ellis wrote a book titled *How to Stubbornly Refuse to Make Yourself Miserable about Anything—Yes, Anything* (1988). In it, he asserted that most of our negative feelings about ourselves result from negative messages we communicate to ourselves. His advice is to challenge negative statements you make to yourself and to replace them with constructive intrapersonal communication. Self-sabotage is poisonous; it destroys our motivation to change and grow. We can be as critical of ourselves as others can; in fact, we probably can do more damage to our self-concepts than others can because we are most aware of our vulnerabilities and fears.

Following Ellis' advice, we can affirm our worth, encourage our growth, and fortify our sense of self-worth. Positive self-talk builds motivation and belief in yourself. It is also helpful to interrupt and challenge negative messages from yourself and others. The next time you hear yourself saying, "I can't do...," or someone else says, "You'll never change," challenge the self-defeating message with self-talk. Say out loud to yourself, "I can do it. I will change." Of course, you won't grow and improve if you listen only to praise, particularly if it is less than honest. Real friends can help us identify areas for growth without making us feel bad about ourselves.

In sum, to improve your self-concept, you should create contexts that support growth and change, and seek experiences and settings that foster belief in yourself and the changes you desire. Also, recognize uppers, downers, and vultures in yourself and others, and learn which people and which kinds of communication assist you in achieving your own goals for self-improvement.

If you'd like to try initiating changes in yourself related to the way you communicate interpersonally, complete the activity "Improving Self-Concept" via MindTap for *Communication in Our Lives*.

BEYOND THE CLASSROOM

CLASSROOM MindTap™

Let's take the material in this chapter beyond the classroom by thinking about how what you've learned about personal identity might apply to the workplace, ethical choices, and engagement with the broader world.

1. **Workplace.** We discussed direct definition and identity scripts as two ways that others define who we are and what we are worth during the early years of life. Extend this by asking how those two factors influence identity development on the job. Recall examples of supervisors and coworkers' direct definitions of you or other employees. For example, were you defined as "a good worker" or "a quick learner"? Consider identity scripts that you were given in a particular workplace. What did others tell you about the company or workplace's identity and about how employees in this particular job were supposed to think and act?

Ethics

2. **Ethics.** How does what you learned in this chapter affect ethical choices about parenting? Reflect on the ethical implications of knowing that parents affect children's self-concepts by their choices of direct definitions, identity scripts, and attachment styles. What ethical responsibilities, if any, do parents have regarding their impact on children's self-concepts and self-esteem?

3. **Engagement.** Not all children have the fortune of having parents who are able to nurture them lovingly and help them develop positive self-concepts. In 1964, the United States launched the Head Start Program to help children and their families who have limited resources. Click **WebLink 3.2** to access the National Head Start Program's Website. Spend some time reading this page and following links it provides. Can you identify ways that the program aims to enhance the self-concepts of underprivileged children and their families?

CHAPTER SUMMARY

 Practice and review the content in this chapter.

In this chapter, we explored the self as a process that evolves as we communicate with others over the course of our lives. As we interact with others, we learn and internalize social perspectives, both those of particular others and those of the generalized other, or society as a whole. Reflected appraisals, direct definitions, and social comparisons are key communication processes that shape how we see ourselves and how we change over time. The perspective of the generalized other includes social views of key aspects of identity, including gender, race, and sexual orientation. However, these are arbitrary social constructions that we may challenge and resist

once we are adults. When we resist social views and values that we consider unethical, we promote change in both society and ourselves.

In the final section of the chapter, we focused on ways to enhance communication competence by improving self-concept. Guidelines include making a firm commitment to personal growth, gaining knowledge about desired changes and the skills they involve, setting realistic goals, accepting yourself as in process, and creating contexts that support the changes you seek. We can make amazing changes in who we are and how we feel about ourselves when we commit to doing so.

APPLYING COMMUNICATION IN OUR LIVES

 MindTap

Communication in Our Lives is supported by a MindTap, a new online learning platform that delivers content, assignments, and a tailored presentation of the course curriculum created by your instructor. MindTap combines all of your learning tools–readings, multimedia, activities and assessments–into a singular learning unit that guides you through the course. Practice

and Present, a unique tool within MindTap, allows you to upload your speech video files for practice or for a grade, comment on your peer's speeches and review your grades. MindTap also includes Speech Builder Express, a powerful tool that guides you through the speech outline and preparation process. For more information or to access MindTap, visit cengagebrain.com.

DEFINITIONS OF KEY CONCEPTS

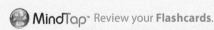 MindTap Review your **Flashcards**.

attachment style Any of several patterns of attachment that result from particular parenting styles that teach children who they are, who others are, and how to approach relationships.

direct definition Communication that explicitly tells us who we are by specifically labeling us and reacting to our behaviors. Direct definition usually occurs first in families and then in interaction with peers and others.

ego boundaries A person's internal sense of where he or she stops and the rest of the world begins.

identity script A guide to action based on rules for living and identity. Initially communicated in families, identity scripts define our roles, how we are to play them, and basic elements in the plot of our lives.

particular others One source of social perspectives that people use to define themselves and guide how they think, act, and feel. The perspectives of particular others are the viewpoints of people who are significant to the self.

perspective of the generalized other The collection of rules, roles, and attitudes endorsed by the whole social community in which we live.

reflected appraisal Our perceptions of others' views of us.

self A multidimensional process in which the individual forms and acts from social perspectives that arise and evolve in communication with himself or herself.

self-disclosure Revelation of information about ourselves that others are unlikely to discover on their own.

self-sabotage Self-talk that communicates that we're no good, we can't do something, we can't change, and so forth. Undermines belief in ourselves and motivation to change and grow.

social comparison Comparing ourselves with others to form judgments of our own talents, abilities, qualities, and so forth.

FOR FURTHER REFLECTION AND DISCUSSION

1. Set one specific goal for personal growth as a communicator. Be sure to specify your goal in terms of clear behavioral changes and make it realistic. As you study different topics during the semester, apply what you learn to your personal goal.

2. What ethical issues do you perceive in the process of developing and continuously refining self-concepts, both your own and those of people around you? Is it as important to be ethical in communicating with yourself (self-talk, or intrapersonal communication) as in communicating with others?

Ethics

3. How do people you meet and get to know on the Internet affect your sense of who you are? Are they significant for you? Do they represent the generalized other to you? Is it useful to distinguish between the impact of face-to-face and online communication?

4. In what ways are your own experiences and your sense of identity consistent with generalizations about the effects on self-concept of race or ethnicity, economic class, sexual orientation, and sex? In what ways do your experiences and your sense of identity diverge from generalizations? What in your own life might account for the instances in which you do not fit generalizations?

5. Historically, India classified people according to caste, one of the most rigid systems of social class. To learn about how a person's caste affected his or her opportunities in life, click **WebLink 3.3**.

SHARPEN YOUR SKILL

1. Reflecting on Your Identity Scripts

Recall identity scripts your parents communicated about who you were or were supposed to become. Can you hear them saying, "Our people do . . ." or "Our family doesn't . . ."? Can you recall messages that told you what and who they expected you to be? As a youngster, did you hear, "You'll go to college" or "You're going to be a doctor"?

Now review key identity scripts. Which ones make sense to you today? Are you still following any that are irrelevant to your present life or that are at odds with your personal values and goals? If so, then commit to changing scripts that aren't productive for you or that conflict with values you hold. You can rewrite identity scripts now that you're an adult.

For additional insight into identity scripts that were communicated to you, complete the activity "Identifying Your Identity Scripts" via MindTap for *Communication in Our Lives.*

2. Your Looking-Glass Self

Identify three people who have been or are particularly important to you. For each person, identify one self-perception you have that reflects the appraisal of you communicated by that person.

Now imagine that you'd never known each of the three people. Describe how you would be different. How would your self-image change?

For instance, Shennoa (see commentary, p.58) might think she would be less independent had her grandmother not influenced how she sees herself.

Trace the way you see yourself to the appraisals that particular others have reflected.

Prepare a 2-minute presentation in which you describe one of the people you've identified as a looking glass for yourself. Explain how this person has influenced the way you see yourself. You may want to look ahead to Part III of this book for guidelines on preparing a speech.

EXPERIENCING COMMUNICATION IN OUR LIVES   MindTap

CASE STUDY: *Parental Teachings*

© Cengage Learning

A video of the conversation scripted here is featured in your Chapter 3 MindTap for *Communication in Our Lives.* Select "Parental Teachings" to watch the video. Improve your own communication skills by reading, watching, and analyzing this communication encounter.

Kate McDonald is in the neighborhood park with her two children, 7-year-old Emma and 5-year-old Jeremy. The three of them walk into the park and approach the swing set.

KATE: Jeremy, why don't you push Emma so she can swing? Emma, you hang on tight.

Jeremy begins pushing his sister, who squeals with delight. Jeremy gives an extra-hard push that lands him in the dirt in front of the swing set. Laughing, Emma jumps off, falling in the dirt beside her brother.

KATE: Come here, sweetie. You've got dirt all over your knees and your pretty new dress.

Kate brushes the dirt off Emma, who then runs over to the jungle gym set that Jeremy is now climbing. Kate smiles as she watches Jeremy climb fearlessly on the bars.

KATE: You're a brave little man, aren't you? How high can you go?

Encouraged by his mother, Jeremy climbs to the top bars and holds up a fist, screaming, "Look at me, Mom! I'm king of the hill! I climbed to the very top!"

Kate laughs and claps her hands to applaud him. Jealous of the attention Jeremy is getting, Emma runs over to the jungle gym and starts climbing. Kate calls out, "Careful, honey. Don't go any higher. You could fall and hurt yourself." When Emma ignores her mother and reaches for a higher bar, Kate walks over and pulls her off, saying, "Emma, I told you that is dangerous. Time to get down. Why don't you play on the swings some more?"

Once Kate puts Emma on the ground, the girl walks over to the swings and begins swaying.

QUESTIONS FOR ANALYSIS AND DISCUSSION   MindTap™

You can answer these questions and see my responses to them online via MindTap for Chapter 3.

1. Identify examples of direct definition in this scenario. How does Kate define Emma and Jeremy?

2. Identify examples of reflected appraisal in this scenario. What appraisals of her son and daughter does Kate reflect to them?

3. What do Emma's and Jeremy's responses to Kate suggest about their acceptance of her views of them?

4. To what extent does Kate's communication with her children reflect conventional gender expectations in Western culture?

Deborah Tannen

Deborah Tannen (1945–), Professor of Linguistics at Georgetown University, was born in Brooklyn, New York. Tannen has written widely about communication across cultural, class, ethnic, and sexual divides. This includes such popular periodicals as the New York Times *magazine,* New York *magazine, and the* Washington Post. *She shares her research with the general public in newspapers, articles, and best-selling books, including* That's Not What I Meant! *(1986) and* You Just Don't Understand: Women and Men in Conversation *(1990).*

"Sex, Lies, and Conversation" originally appeared in the Washington Post *in 1990 in conjunction with the publication of "You Just Don't Understand." Both present the difficulties men and women have in communicating with one another.*

Sex, Lies and Conversation; Why Is It So Hard for Men and Women to Talk to Each Other? *(1994)*

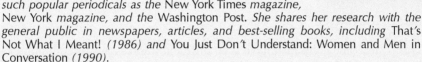

I was addressing a small gathering in a suburban Virginia living room—a women's group that had invited men to join them. Throughout the evening, one man had been particularly talkative, frequently offering ideas and anecdotes, while his wife sat silently beside him on the couch. Toward the end of the evening, I commented that women frequently complain that their husbands don't talk to them. This man quickly concurred. He gestured toward his wife and said, "She's the talker in our family." The room burst into laughter; the man looked puzzled and hurt. "It's true," he explained. "When I come home from work I have nothing to say. If she didn't keep the conversation going, we'd spend the whole evening in silence."

This episode crystallizes the irony that although American men tend to talk more than women in public situations, they often talk less at home. And this pattern is wreaking havoc with marriage.

The pattern was observed by political scientist Andrew Hacker in the late '70s. Sociologist Catherine Kohler Riessman reports in her new book *Divorce Talk* that most of the women she interviewed—but only a few of the men—gave lack of communication as the reason for their divorces. Given the current divorce rate of nearly 50 percent, that amounts to millions of cases in the United States every year—a virtual epidemic of failed conversation.

In my own research, complaints from women about their husbands most often focused not on tangible inequities such as having given up the chance for a career to accompany a husband to his, or doing far more than their share of daily life-support work like cleaning, cooking, social arrangements and errands. Instead, they focused on communication: "He doesn't listen to me," "He doesn't talk to me." I found, as Hacker observed years before, that most wives want their husbands to be, first and foremost, conversational partners, but few husbands share this expectation of their wives.

5 In short, the image that best represents the current crisis is the stereotypical cartoon scene of a man sitting at the breakfast table with a newspaper held up in front of his face, while a woman glares at the back of it, wanting to talk.

LINGUISTIC BATTLE OF THE SEXES

How can women and men have such different impressions of communication in marriage? Why the widespread imbalance in their interests and expectations?

In the April [1990] issue of *American Psychologist,* Stanford University's Eleanor Maccoby reports the results of her own and others' research showing that children's development is most influenced by the social structure of peer interactions. Boys and girls tend to play with children of their own gender, and their sex-separate groups have different organizational structures and interactive norms.

I believe these systematic differences in childhood socialization make talk between women and men like cross-cultural communication, heir to all the attraction and pitfalls of that enticing but difficult enterprise. My research on men's and women's conversations uncovered patterns similar to those described for children's groups.

For women, as for girls, intimacy is the fabric of relationships, and talk is the thread from which it is woven. Little girls create and maintain friendships by exchanging secrets; similarly, women regard conversation as the cornerstone of friendship. So a woman expects her husband to be a new and improved version of a best friend. What is important is not the individual subjects that are discussed but the sense of closeness, of a life shared, that emerges when people tell their thoughts, feelings, and impressions.

10 Bonds between boys can be as intense as girls', but they are based less on talking, more on doing things together. Since they don't assume talk is the cement that binds a relationship, men don't know what kind of talk women want, and they don't miss it when it isn't there.

Boys' groups are larger, more inclusive, and more hierarchical, so boys must struggle to avoid the subordinate position in the group. This may play a role in women's complaints that men don't listen to them. Some men really don't like to listen, because being the listener makes them feel one-down, like a child listening to adults or an employee to a boss.

But often when women tell men, "You aren't listening," and the men protest, "I am," the men are right. The impression of not listening results from misalignments in the mechanics of conversation. The misalignment begins as soon as a man and a woman take physical positions. This became clear when I studied videotapes made by psychologist Bruce Dorval of children and adults talking to their same-sex best friends. I found that at every age, the girls and women faced each other directly, their eyes anchored on each other's faces. At every age, the boys and men sat at angles to each other and looked elsewhere in the room, periodically glancing at each other. They were obviously attuned to each other, often mirroring each other's movements. But the tendency of men to face away can give women the impression they aren't listening even when they are. A young woman in college was frustrated: Whenever she told her boyfriend she wanted to talk to him, he would lie down on the floor, close his eyes, and put his arm over his face. This signaled to her, "He's taking a nap." But he insisted he was listening extra hard. Normally, he looks around the room, so he is easily distracted. Lying down and covering his eyes helped him concentrate on what she was saying.

Analogous to the physical alignment that women and men take in conversation is their topical alignment. The girls in my study tended to talk at length about one topic, but the boys tended to jump from topic to topic. The second-grade girls exchanged stories about people they knew. The second-grade boys teased, told jokes, noticed things in the room and talked about finding games to play. The sixth-grade girls talked about problems with a mutual friend. The sixth-grade boys talked about 55 different topics, none of which extended over more than a few turns.

LISTENING TO BODY LANGUAGE

Switching topics is another habit that gives women the impression men aren't listening, especially if they switch to a topic about themselves. But the evidence of the 10th-grade boys in my study indicates otherwise. The 10th-grade boys sprawled across their chairs with bodies parallel and eyes straight ahead, rarely looking at each other. They looked as if they were riding in a car, staring out the windshield. But they were talking about their feelings. One boy was upset because a girl had told him he had a drinking problem, and the other was feeling alienated from all his friends.

Now, when a girl told a friend about a problem, the friend responded by asking probing questions and expressing agreement and understanding. But the boys dismissed each other's problems. Todd assured Richard that his drinking was "no big problem" because "sometimes you're funny when you're off your butt." And when Todd said he felt left out, Richard responded, "Why should you? You know more people than me."

Women perceived such responses as belittling and unsupportive. But the boys seemed satisfied with them. Whereas women reassure each other by implying, "You shouldn't feel bad because I've had similar experiences," men do so by implying, "You shouldn't feel bad because your problems aren't so bad."

There are even simpler reasons for women's impression that men don't listen. Linguist Lynette Hirschman found that women make more listener-noise, such as "mhm," "uhuh," and "yeah," to show "I'm with you." Men, she found, more often give silent attention. Women who expect a stream of listener-noise interpret silent attention as no attention at all.

Women's conversational habits are as frustrating to men as men's are to women. Men who expect silent attention interpret a stream of listener-noise as overreaction or impatience. Also, when women talk to each other in a

15

close, comfortable setting, they often overlap, finish each other's sentences and anticipate what the other is about to say. This practice, which I call "participatory listenership," is often perceived by men as interruption, intrusion and lack of attention.

A parallel difference caused a man to complain about his wife, "She just wants to talk about her own point of view. If I show her another view, she gets mad at me." When most women talk to each other, they assume a conversationalist's job is to express agreement and support. But many men see their conversational duty as pointing out the other side of an argument. This is heard as disloyalty by women, and refusal to offer the requisite support. It is not that women don't want to see other points of view, but that they prefer them phrased as suggestions and inquiries rather than as direct challenges.

20 In his book *Fighting for Life,* Walter Ong points out that men use "agonistic" or warlike, oppositional formats to do almost anything; thus discussion becomes debate, and conversation a competitive sport. In contrast, women see conversation as a ritual means of establishing rapport. If Jane tells a problem and June says she has a similar one, they walk away feeling closer to each other. But this attempt at establishing rapport can backfire when used with men. Men take too literally women's ritual "troubles talk," just as women mistake men's ritual challenges for real attack.

THE SOUNDS OF SILENCE

These differences begin to clarify why women and men have such different expectations about communication in marriage. For women, talk creates intimacy. Marriage is an orgy of closeness: you can tell your feelings and thoughts, and still be loved. Their greatest fear is being pushed away. But men live in a hierarchical world, where talk maintains independence and status. They are on guard to protect themselves from being put down and pushed around.

This explains the paradox of the talkative man who said of his silent wife, "She's the talker." In the public setting of a guest lecture, he felt challenged to show his intelligence and display his understanding of the lecture. But at home, where he has nothing to prove and no one to defend against, he is free to remain silent. For his wife, being home means she is free from the worry that something she says might offend someone, or spark disagreement, or appear to be showing off; at home she is free to talk.

The communication problems that endanger marriage can't be fixed by mechanical engineering. They require a new conceptual framework about the role of talk in human relationships. Many of the psychological explanations that have become second nature may not be helpful, because they tend to blame either women (for not being assertive enough) or men (for not being in touch with their feelings). A sociolinguistic approach by which male-female conversation is seen as cross-cultural communication allows us to understand the problem and forge solutions without blaming either party.

Once the problem is understood, improvement comes naturally, as it did to the young woman and her boyfriend who seemed to go to sleep when she wanted to talk. Previously, she had accused him of not listening, and he had refused to change his behavior, since that would be admitting fault. But then she learned about and explained to him the differences in women's and men's habitual ways of aligning themselves in conversation. The next time she told him she wanted to talk, he began, as usual, by lying down and covering his eyes. When the familiar negative reaction bubbled up, she reassured herself that he really was listening. But then he sat up and looked at her. Thrilled she asked why. He said, "You like me to look at you when we talk, so I'll try to do it." Once he saw their differences as cross-cultural rather than right and wrong, he independently altered his behavior.

Women who feel abandoned and deprived when their husbands won't   25 listen to or report daily news may be happy to discover their husbands trying to adapt once they understand the place of small talk in women's relationships. But if their husbands don't adapt, the women may still be comforted that for men, this is not a failure of intimacy. Accepting the difference, the wives may look to their friends or family for that kind of talk. And husbands who can't provide it shouldn't feel their wives have made unreasonable demands. Some couples will still decide to divorce, but at least their decisions will be based on realistic expectations.

In these times of resurgent ethnic conflicts, the world desperately needs cross-cultural understanding. Like charity, successful cross-cultural communication should begin at home.

Speaking in Tongues: Does Language Unify or Divide Us?

The diverse voices in the previous chapters reflect some of the numerous ethnic and racial aspects of the new American mosaic—as well as global perceptions of American exceptionalism. Part of this mosaic is the variety of languages we hear on American streets and college campuses. Of course, you have been taught to speak and write the same language—that standard variety of English that places you in the college classroom today. Knowing the standard English "code" provides you with a powerful tool, offering pragmatic and liberating ways to gain control over your world.

However, other languages might compete for your attention at home or in your community. Powerful constituencies—politicians and advertisers among them—exploit this fact. For example, some Anglo politicians try to speak Spanish to Latino crowds (often to the amusement of native Spanish speakers). Other constituencies, threatened by our multilingual world, try to enact "English-only" laws in various states. Moreover, governments often use language—for example, words like "patriotism" or "Islamic fascism"—to advance political goals. Language can unify or divide a community or nation, but basically it remains a mark of your identity. To know a language or languages permits you to navigate your community, culture, and even global society.

Imagine, for example, what it would be like if you were illiterate. For one thing, you wouldn't be in college. You might not be able to read a menu or fill out a job application. You might not be interested in voting because you cannot read the names of the candidates. Illiteracy in reality is common around the world—and far more common in the United States than you might think.

We have vivid reminders of both the cost of illiteracy and also the power of literacy in film and literature. In the film *Driving Miss Daisy*, the character played by Morgan Freeman goes through most of his life pretending to read the daily newspaper. When Daisy (played by

The neighborhood of Elmhurst, Queens, in New York City, is one of the most ethnically and linguistically diverse places in the world. At Elmhurst's Newtown High School alone, students come from more than 100 countries and at least 39 languages are spoken. In this photograph, local schoolchildren take part in the neighborhood's annual International Day Festival on May 27, 1999.

Thinking About the Image

1. Recall a class photograph from your childhood. Was your school as diverse as this group of schoolchildren, or not? What are the advantages of being exposed to so many nationalities and languages at such a young age? What are the disadvantages?
2. News photographers often shoot many images of the same event, sometimes even multiple rolls of film, and then decide with their editors which unique image best captures the spirit of the event. Why do you think this photo was selected?
3. Are there parades for various ethnic or social groups in your community? How are those events covered in the local news media?
4. Would this parade have achieved its purpose, or appealed to its audience, as effectively if the marchers were adults instead of children? Why or why not? Would the message (or purpose) have been different? In what way?

Jessica Tandy) teaches him to read, his world—and his comprehension of it—expands. Or consider one of the memorable sequences in *The Autobiography of Malcolm X*. Malcolm teaches himself to read and write when he is in prison. He starts at the beginning of the dictionary and works his way to the end. Going into prison as Richard Little, he comes out as Malcolm X, his identity reconstructed not only by the acquisition of a new system of belief—Islam—but also by a newly acquired literacy. In his writing and in his recovered life, Malcolm X harnessed the power of language to transform himself and his understanding of the world.

Think of language, then, as a radical weapon. Language permits you to share experiences and emotions, process information, analyze situations and events, defend a position, advocate a cause, and make decisions. Language contributes to the growth of the self. Language is the bedrock of our academic, social, and professional lives. Language is a liberating force—but some writers in this chapter remind us that language can also be culturally and politically divisive.

The idea that language is the key to our identity and our perception of the world is not new. Early Greek and Roman philosophers believed that you could not be a good thinker or writer unless you were a good person. Assuming that you are a good person, you possess a repertoire of mental skills that you can bring to bear on various situations and dimensions of your life. You can draw inferences, interpret conditions, understand causal relationships, develop arguments, make intelligent choices, and so forth. But have you ever found yourself in a situation where you know what you mean but not how to say it? Or think of how difficult it must be for people acquiring a second language; they know what they mean in their primary language but cannot express it in their new one. The essays in this chapter deal with precisely this situation.

The writers in this chapter illuminate the power and paradox of language. They link language, culture, politics, and identity. They use language with skill intelligence, and emotion. They work with the problems and contradictions of language, seeking answers to the question, Who am I, and where do my words—my languages—fit into the American as well as the world mosaic?

Leave Your Name at the Border

Manuel Munoz

Manuel Munoz, who was born in 1972 in Dinuba, California, has written two well-received collections of short fiction, *Zigzagger* (2003) and *The Faith Healer of Olive Avenue* (2007), inspired by his childhood in the San Joaquin Valley. The son of farmworkers in California's Central Valley, Munoz was the first person in his family to go to college, receiving a B.A. from Harvard University and an M.F.A. from Cornell University. The recipient of a National Endowment for the Arts fellowship in fiction and the Whiting Writers' Award, Munoz contributes stories and essays to periodicals including the *Boston Review*, *Edinburgh Review*, and *The New York Times*. In this article from the August 1, 2007, issue of *The New York Times*, Munoz discusses the problems and power of code-switching as he ponders the ways in which various constituencies perceive him—and his name.

Before Reading

Do you have an immigrant name, a mainstream or assimilated name, or something in between? Is your name "white" or "not white"? What do you think your name—first or last—tells others about who you are and where you are from?

A t the Fresno airport, as I made my way to the gate, I heard a name over the intercom. The way the name was pronounced by the gate agent made me want to see what she looked like. That is, I wanted to see whether she was Mexican. Around Fresno, identity politics rarely deepen into exacting terms, so to say "Mexican" means, essentially, "not white." The slivered self-identifications Chicano, Hispanic, Mexican-American and Latino are not part of everyday life in the Valley. You're either Mexican or you're not. If someone wants to know if you were born in Mexico, they'll ask. Then you're From Over There—de allá. And leave it at that.

The gate agent, it turned out, was Mexican. Well-coiffed, in her 30s, she wore foundation that was several shades lighter than the rest of her skin. It was the kind of makeup job I've learned to silently identify at the mall when I'm with my mother, who will say nothing about it until we're back in the car. Then she'll point to the darkness of her own skin, wondering aloud why women try to camouflage who they are.

I watched the Mexican gate agent busy herself at the counter, professional and studied. Once again, she picked up the microphone and, with authority, announced the name of the missing customer: "Eugenio Reyes, please come to the front desk."

You can probably guess how she said it. Her Anglicized pronunciation wouldn't be unusual in a place like California's Central Valley. I didn't have a Mexican name there either: I was an instruction guide.

When people ask me where I'm from, I say Fresno because I don't expect them to know little Dinuba. Fresno is a booming city of nearly 500,000 these days, with a diversity—white, Mexican, African-American,

Armenian, Hmong and Middle Eastern people are all well represented—that shouldn't surprise anyone. It's in the small towns like Dinuba that surround Fresno that the awareness of cultural difference is stripped down to the interactions between the only two groups that tend to live there: whites and Mexicans. When you hear a Mexican name spoken in these towns, regardless of the speaker's background, it's no wonder that there's an "English way of pronouncing it."

I was born in 1972, part of a generation that learned both English and   6
Spanish. Many of my cousins and siblings are bilingual, serving as translators for those in the family whose English is barely functional. Others have no way of following the Spanish banter at family gatherings. You can tell who falls into which group: Estella, Eric, Delia, Dubina, Melanie. It's intriguing to watch "American" names begin to dominate among my nieces and nephews and second cousins, as well as with the children of my hometown friends. I am not surprised to meet 5-year-old Brandon or Kaitlyn. Hardly anyone questions the incongruity of matching these names with last names like Trujillo or Zepeda. The English-only way of life partly explains the quiet erasure of cultural difference that assimilation has attempted to accomplish. A name like Kaitlyn Zepeda doesn't completely obscure her ethnicity, but the half-step of her name, as a gesture, is almost understandable.

Spanish was and still is viewed with suspicion: Always the language of   7
the vilified illegal immigrant, it segregated schoolchildren into English-only and bilingual programs; it defined you, above all else, as part of a lower class. Learning English, though, brought its own complications. It was simultaneously the language of the white population and a path toward the richer, expansive identity of "American." But it took getting out of the Valley for me to understand that "white" and "American" were two very different things.

Something as simple as saying our names "in English" was our   8
unwittingly complicit gesture of trying to blend in. Pronouncing Mexican names correctly was never encouraged. Names like Daniel, Olivia and Marco slipped right into the mutability of the English language. I remember a school ceremony at which the mathematics teacher, a white man, announced the names of Mexican students correctly and caused some confusion, if not embarrassment. Years later we recognized that he spoke in deference to our Spanish-speaking parents in the audience, caring teacher that he was.

These were difficult names for a non-Spanish speaker: Araceli,   9
Nadira, Luis (a beautiful name when you glide the u and the i as you're supposed to). We had been accustomed to having our birth names altered for convenience. Concepción was Connie. Ramón was Raymond. My cousin Esperanza was Hope—but her name was pronounced "Hopie"

because any Spanish speaker would automatically pronounce the e at the end.

Ours, then, were names that stood as barriers to a complete embrace 10 of an American identity, simply because their pronunciations required a slip into Spanish, the otherness that assimilation was supposed to erase. What to do with names like Amado, Lucio or Élida? There are no English "equivalents," no answer when white teachers asked, "What does your name mean?" when what they really wanted to know was "What's the English one?" So what you heard was a name butchered beyond recognition, a pronunciation that pointed the finger at the Spanish language as the source of clunky sound and ugly rhythm.

My stepfather, from Ojos de Agua, Mexico, jokes when I ask him 11 about the names of Mexicans born here. He deliberately stumbles over pronunciations, imitating our elders who have difficulty with Bradley and Madelyn. "Ashley Sánchez. ¿Tú crees?" He wonders aloud what has happened to the "nombres del rancho"—traditional Mexican names that are hardly given anymore to children born in the States: Heraclio, Madaleno, Otilia, Dominga. My stepfather's experience with the Anglicization of his name—Antonio to Tony—ties into something bigger than learning English. For him, the erasure of his name was about deference and subservience. Becoming Tony gave him a measure of access as he struggled to learn English and get more fieldwork.

This isn't to say that my stepfather welcomed the change, only that 12 he could not put up much resistance. Not changing put him at risk of being passed over for work. English was a world of power and decisions, of smooth, uninterrupted negotiation. Clear communication meant you could go unsupervised. Every gesture made toward convincing an employer that English was on its way to being mastered had the potential to make a season of fieldwork profitable. It's curious that many of us growing up in Dinuba adhered to the same rules. Although as children of farm workers we worked in the fields at an early age, we'd also had the opportunity to stay in one town long enough to finish school. Most of us had learned English early and splintered off into a dual existence of English at school, Spanish at home. But instead of recognizing the need for fluency in both languages, we turned it into a peculiar kind of battle. English was for public display. Spanish was for privacy—and privacy quickly turned to shame. The corrosive effect of assimilation is the displacement of one culture over another, the inability to sustain more than one way of being. It isn't a code word for racial and ethnic acculturation only. It applies to needing to belong, of seeing from the outside and wondering how to get in and then, once inside, realizing there are always those still on the fringe.

When I went to college on the East Coast, I was confronted for the 13
first time by people who said my name correctly without prompting; if
they stumbled, there was a quick apology and an honest plea to help
with the pronunciation. But introducing myself was painful: already
shy, I avoided meeting people because I didn't want to say my name, felt
burdened by my own history. I knew that my small-town upbringing and
its limitations on Spanish would not have been tolerated by any of the
students of color who had grown up in large cities, in places where the
sheer force of their native languages made them dominant in their neighborhoods. It didn't take long for me to assert the power of code-switching
in public, the transferring of words from one language to another, regardless of who might be listening. I was learning that the English language
composed new meanings when its constrictions were ignored, crossed
over or crossed out. Language is all about manipulation, or not listening
to the rules.

When I come back to Dinuba, I have a hard time hearing my name said 14
incorrectly, but I have an even harder time beginning a conversation with
others about why the pronunciation of our names matters. Leaving a small
town requires an embrace of a larger point of view, but a town like Dinuba
remains forever embedded in an either/or way of life. My stepfather still
answers to Tony and, as the United States–born children grow older, their
Anglicized names begin to signify who does and who does not "belong"—
who was born here and who is de allá.

My name is Manuel. To this day, most people cannot say it correctly,
the way it was intended to be said. But I can live with that because I love
the alliteration of my full name. It wasn't the name my mother, Esmeralda, 15
was going to give me. At the last minute, my father named me after an
uncle I would never meet. My name was to have been Ricardo. Growing
up in Dinuba, I'm certain I would have become Ricky or even Richard, and
the journey toward the discovery of the English language's extraordinary
power in even the most ordinary of circumstances would probably have
gone unlearned.

I count on a collective sense of cultural loss to once again swing the 16
names back to our native language. The Mexican gate agent announced
Eugenio Reyes, but I never got a chance to see who appeared. I pictured an
older man, cowboy hat in hand, but I made the assumption on his name
alone, the clash of privileges I imagined between someone de allá and a
Mexican woman with a good job in the United States. Would she speak to
him in Spanish? Or would she raise her voice to him as if he were hard of
hearing?

But who was I to imagine this man being from anywhere, based on his name alone? At a place of arrivals and departures, it sank into me that the currency of our names is a stroke of luck: because mine was not an easy name, it forced me to consider how language would rule me if I allowed it. Yet I discovered that only by leaving. My stepfather must live in the Valley, a place that does not allow that choice, every day. And Eugenio Reyes— I do not know if he was coming or going. 17

Thinking About the Essay

1. Why do you think that Munoz begins his essay—and ends it as well—at the Fresno, California, airport? On what and whom does he focus, and how does this focus serve to illuminate his broader analysis?

2. What is Munoz's thesis, and where does he state it? How does the "corrosive effect of assimilation" inform this thesis?

3. Munoz organizes this essay around a series of contrasts. What is the primary contrast? What are additional contrasts that inform this comparative structure?

4. Why does Munoz introduce so many names in this essay—sometimes lists of names as in paragraphs 6 and 9? Do you find these names to be a distraction or do they reinforce the writer's thesis? Explain.

5. Explain the ways in which Munoz merges narrative, personal experience, analysis, and perhaps even argument in this essay. What does his strategy tell you about mixing modes or patterns when writing an essay?

Responding in Writing

6. Write a personal essay about your own name, combining narrative, descriptive, and expository techniques.

7. Write an analytical paper on what Munoz terms "the power of code-switching in public" (paragraph 13).

8. Argue for or against the proposition that assimilation can have a corrosive effect.

Networking

9. In groups of three or four, develop a list of all the names—and variants of names—that Munoz introduces in his essay. Discuss the relevance of these names to Munoz's argument. Appoint one member of the group to present your evaluation.

10. Go online and find out more about "code-switching." Provide a critique of your research in a brief paper.

Mother Tongue

AMY TAN

Amy Tan was born in San Francisco, California, in 1952, only two and a half years after her parents emigrated from China to the United States. She was educated at San Jose State University and the University of California at Berkeley and then worked as a reporter and technical writer. Tan is best known as a novelist whose fiction focuses on the conflict in culture between Chinese parents and their Americanized children. Her first novel, *The Joy Luck Club* (1989), was highly popular and adapted by Hollywood as a feature film. Tan's other novels are *The Kitchen God's Wife* (1991), *The Hundred Secret Senses* (1995), *The Bonesetter's Daughter* (2001), and *Saving the Fish from Drowning* (2006). Tan published a nonfiction work, *The Opposite of Fate: A Book of Musings*, in 2003. Tan's complicated relationship with her mother, Daisy, who died of Alzheimer's disease in 1999 at the age of eighty-three, is central to much of her fiction. In this essay, published in 1990 in *The Threepenny Review*, Tan, who has a master's degree in linguistics, invokes her mother in exploring the "Englishes" that immigrants employ as they navigate American culture.

Before Reading

How many "Englishes" do you speak, and what types of English do you speak in various situations? Is the English you speak in the classroom the same as you speak in your home or dormitory?

I am not a scholar of English or literature. I cannot give you much more   1
than personal opinions on the English language and its variations in this country or others.

I am a writer. And by that definition, I am someone who has always   2
loved language. I am fascinated by language in daily life. I spend a great deal of my time thinking about the power of language—the way it can evoke an emotion, a visual image, a complex idea, or a simple truth. Language is the tool of my trade. And I use them all—all the Englishes I grew up with.

Recently, I was made keenly aware of the different Englishes I do   3
use. I was giving a talk to a large group of people, the same talk I had

already given to half a dozen other groups. The nature of the talk was about my writing, my life, and my book, *The Joy Luck Club*. The talk was going along well enough, until I remembered one major difference that made the whole talk sound wrong. My mother was in the room. And it was perhaps the first time she had heard me give a lengthy speech, using the kind of English I have never used with her. I was saying things like, "The intersection of memory upon imagination" and "There is an aspect of my fiction that relates to thus-and-thus"—a speech filled with carefully wrought grammatical phrases, burdened, it suddenly seemed to me, with nominalized forms, past perfect tenses, conditional phrases, all the forms of standard English that I had learned in school and through books, the forms of English I did not use at home with my mother.

Just last week, I was walking down the street with my mother, and I again found myself conscious of the English I was using, the English I do use with her. We were talking about the price of new and used furniture and I heard myself saying this: "Not waste money that way." My husband was with us as well, and he didn't notice any switch in my English. And then I realized why. It's because over the twenty years we've been together I've often used that same kind of English with him, and sometimes he even uses it with me. It has become our language of intimacy, a different sort of English that relates to family talk, the language I grew up with.

So you'll have some idea of what this family talk I heard sounds like, I'll quote what my mother said during a recent conversation which I videotaped and then transcribed. During this conversation, my mother was talking about a political gangster in Shanghai who had the same last name as her family's, Du, and how the gangster in his early years wanted to be adopted by her family, which was rich by comparison. Later, the gangster became more powerful, far richer than my mother's family, and one day showed up at my mother's wedding to pay his respects. Here's what she said in part:

"Du Yusong having business like fruit stand. Like off the street kind. He is Du like Du Zong—but not Tsung-ming Island people. The local people call putong, the river east side, he belong to that side local people. That man want to ask Du Zong father take him in like become own family. Du Zong father wasn't look down on him, but didn't take seriously, until that man big like become a mafia. Now important person, very hard to inviting him. Chinese way, came only to show respect, don't stay for dinner. Respect for making big celebration, he shows up. Mean gives lots of respect. Chinese custom. Chinese social life that way. If too important won't have to stay too long. He come to my wedding. I didn't see, I heard it. I gone to boy's side, they have YMCA dinner. Chinese age I was nineteen."

You should know that my mother's expressive command of English belies how much she actually understands. She reads the *Forbes* report, listens to *Wall Street Week,* converses daily with her stockbroker, and reads all of Shirley MacLaine's books with ease—all kinds of things I can't begin to understand. Yet some of my friends tell me they understand 50 percent of what my mother says. Some say they understand 80 to 90 percent. Some say they understand none of it, as if she were speaking pure Chinese. But to me, my mother's English is perfectly clear, perfectly natural. It's my mother tongue. Her language, as I hear it, is vivid, direct, full of observation and imagery. That was the language that helped shape the way I saw things, expressed things, made sense of the world.   7

Lately, I've been giving more thought to the kind of English my mother speaks. Like others, I have described it to people as "broken" or "fractured" English. But I wince when I say that. It has always bothered me that I can think of no way to describe it other than "broken," as if it were damaged and needed to be fixed, as if it lacked a certain wholeness and soundness. I've heard other terms used, "limited English," for example. But they seem just as bad, as if everything is limited, including people's perceptions of the limited English speaker.   8

I know this for a fact, because when I was growing up, my mother's "limited" English limited *my* perception of her. I was ashamed of her English. I believed that her English reflected the quality of what she had to say. That is, because she expressed them imperfectly her thoughts were imperfect. And I had plenty of empirical evidence to support me: the fact that people in department stores, at banks, and at restaurants did not take her seriously, did not give her good service, pretended not to understand her, or even acted as if they did not hear her.   9

My mother has long realized the limitations of her English as well. When I was fifteen, she used to have me call people on the phone to pretend I was she. In this guise, I was forced to ask for information or even to complain and yell at people who had been rude to her. One time it was a call to her stockbroker in New York. She had cashed out her small portfolio and it just so happened we were going to go to New York the next week, our very first trip outside California. I had to get on the phone and say in an adolescent voice that was not very convincing, "This is Mrs. Tan."   10

And my mother was standing in the back whispering loudly, "Why he don't send me check, already two weeks late. So mad he lie to me, losing me money." 11

And then I said in perfect English, "Yes, I'm getting rather concerned. You had agreed to send the check two weeks ago, but it hasn't arrived." 12

Then she began to talk more loudly. "What he want, I come to New York tell him front of his boss, you cheating me?" And I was trying to calm her down, make her be quiet, while telling the stockbroker, "I can't tolerate any more excuses. If I don't receive the check immediately, I am going to have to speak to your manager when I'm in New York next week." And sure enough, the following week there we were in front of this astonished stockbroker, and I was sitting there red-faced and quiet, and my mother, the real Mrs. Tan, was shouting at his boss in her impeccable broken English. 13

We used a similar routine just five days ago, for a situation that was far less humorous. My mother had gone to the hospital for an appointment, to find out about a benign brain tumor a CAT scan had revealed a month ago. She said she had spoken very good English, her best English, no mistakes. Still, she said, the hospital did not apologize when they said they had lost the CAT scan and she had come for nothing. She said they did not seem to have any sympathy when she told them she was anxious to know the exact diagnosis, since her husband and son had both died of brain tumors. She said they would not give her any more information until the next time and she would have to make another appointment for that. So she said she would not leave until the doctor called her daughter. She wouldn't budge. And when the doctor finally called her daughter, me, who spoke in perfect English—lo and behold—we had assurances the CAT scan would be found, promises that a conference call on Monday would be held, and apologies for any suffering my mother had gone through for a most regrettable mistake. 14

I think my mother's English almost had an effect on limiting my possibilities in life as well. Sociologists and linguists probably will tell you that a person's developing language skills are more influenced by peers. But I do think that the language spoken in the family, especially in immigrant families which are more insular, plays a large role in shaping the language of the child. And I believe that it affected my results on achievement tests, IQ tests, and the SAT. While my English skills were never judged as poor, compared to math, English could not be considered my strong suit. In grade school I did moderately well, getting perhaps B's, 15 sometimes B-pluses, in English and scoring perhaps in the sixtieth or seventieth percentile on achievement tests. But those scores were not good enough to override the opinion that my true abilities lay in math and science, because in those areas I achieved A's and scored in the ninetieth percentile or higher.

This was understandable. Math is precise; there is only one correct 16 answer. Whereas, for me at least, the answers on English tests were always a judgment call, a matter of opinion and personal experience. Those tests were constructed around items like fill-in-the-blank sentence completion, such as, "Even though Tom was, Mary thought he was." And the correct answer always seemed to be the most bland combinations of thoughts, for example, "Even though Tom was shy, Mary thought he was charming," with the grammatical structure "even though" limiting the correct answer to some sort of semantic opposites, so you wouldn't get answers like, "Even though Tom was foolish, Mary thought he was ridiculous." Well, according to my mother, there were very few limitations as to what Tom could have been and what Mary might have thought of him. So I never did well on tests like that.

The same was true with word analogies, pairs of words in which 17 you were supposed to find some sort of logical, semantic relationship— for example, "*Sunset* is to *nightfall* as _____ is to _____." And here you would be presented with a list of four possible pairs, one of which showed the same kind of relationship: *red* is to *stoplight, bus* is to *arrival, chills* is to *fever, yawn* is to *boring*. Well, I could never think that way. I knew what the tests were asking, but I could not block out of my mind the images already created by the first pair," *sunset* is to *nightfall*"—and I would see a burst of colors against a darkening sky, the moon rising, the lowering of a curtain of stars. And all the other pairs of words—red, bus, stoplight, boring—just threw up a mass of confusing images, making it impossible for me to sort out something as logical as saying: "A sunset precedes nightfall" is the same as "a chill precedes a fever." The only way I would have gotten that answer right would have been to imagine an associative situation, for example, my being disobedient and staying out past sunset, catching a chill at night, which turns into feverish pneumonia as punishment, which indeed did happen to me.

I have been thinking about all this lately, about my mother's English, 18 about achievement tests. Because lately I've been asked, as a writer, why there are not more Asian Americans represented in American literature. Why are there few Asian Americans enrolled in creative writing programs?

Why do so many Chinese students go into engineering? Well, these are broad sociological questions I can't begin to answer. But I have noticed in surveys—in fact, just last week—that Asian students, as a whole, always do significantly better on math achievement tests than in English. And this makes me think that there are other Asian-American students whose English spoken in the home might also be described as "broken" or "limited." And perhaps they also have teachers who are steering them away from writing and into math and science, which is what happened to me.

Fortunately, I happen to be rebellious in nature and enjoy the challenge of disproving assumptions made about me. I became an English major my first year in college, after being enrolled as pre-med. I started writing non-fiction as a freelancer the week after I was told by my former boss that writing was my worst skill and I should hone my talents toward account management. 19

But it wasn't until 1985 that I finally began to write fiction. And at first I wrote using what I thought to be wittily crafted sentences, sentences that would finally prove I had mastery over the English language. Here's an example from the first draft of a story that later made its way into *The Joy Luck Club*, but without this line: "That was my mental quandary in its nascent state." A terrible line, which I can barely pronounce. 20

Fortunately, for reasons I won't get into today, I later decided I should envision a reader for the stories I would write. And the reader I decided upon was my mother, because these were stories about mothers. So with this reader in mind—and in fact she did read my early drafts—I began to write stories using all the Englishes I grew up with: the English I spoke to my mother, which for lack of a better term might be described as "simple"; the English she used with me, which for lack of a better term might be described as "broken"; my translation of her Chinese, which could certainly be described as "watered down"; and what I imagined to be her translation of her Chinese if she could speak in perfect English, her internal language, and for that I sought to preserve the essence, but neither an English nor a Chinese structure. I wanted to capture what language ability tests can never reveal: her intent, her passion, her imagery, the rhythms of her speech and the nature of her thoughts. 21

Apart from what any critic had to say about my writing, I knew I had succeeded where it counted when my mother finished reading my book and gave me her verdict: "So easy to read." 22

Thinking About the Essay

1. Explain the multiple meanings of Tan's title and how they illuminate the essay. What are the four ways Tan says language can work?

2. What is Tan's thesis, and where does it appear? How do we know her point of view about other "Englishes"? Does she state it directly or indirectly, and where?

3. How do narration and description interact in this essay? How does Tan describe her mother? What is the importance of dialogue?

4. What is Tan's viewpoint about language? Does she state that language should always be "simple"? Why or why not? To the extent that Tan's mother is an intended audience for her essay, is her language simple? Explain your answer by specific reference to her words and sentences. Finally, why does Tan's mother find her daughter's writing easy to understand?

5. How and where does Tan use humor in this essay? Where does Tan employ amusing anecdotes? What is her purpose in presenting these anecdotes, and how do they influence the essay's overall tone?

Responding in Writing

6. Tan suggests that the way we use language reflects the way we see the world. Write an essay based on this observation. Feel free to present an analytical paper or a narrative and descriptive essay, or to blend these patterns as does Tan.

7. Should all Americans speak and write the same language? Answer this question in an argumentative essay.

8. Tan writes about the "shame" she once experienced because of her mother's speech (paragraph 9). Write an essay about the dangers of linking personality or behavior to language. Can this linkage be used to promote racist, sexist, or other discriminatory ideas?

Networking

9. With two other class members, draw up a list of all the "Englishes" you have encountered. For example, how do your parents speak? What about relatives? Friends? Classmates? Personalities on television? Share your list with the class.

10. Conduct Internet or library research on the role of stereotyping by language in American radio and/or film. You might want to look into the popularity of the Charlie Chan series or Amos and Andy, or focus on a particular film that stereotypes a group. Present your information in an analytical and evaluative essay.

Mute in an English-Only World

CHANG-RAE LEE

Chang-rae Lee was born in 1965 in Seoul, South Korea. He and his family emigrated to the United States in 1968. Lee attended public schools in New Rochelle, New York; graduated from Yale University (B.A., 1987); and received an M.F.A. degree from the University of Oregon (1993). His first novel, *Native Speaker* (1995), won several prizes, including the Ernest Hemingway Foundation/PEN Award for First Fiction. He has also written *A Gesture Life* (1999) and *Aloft* (2004), and he has published fiction and nonfiction in many magazines, including *The New Yorker* and *Time*. Lee has taught in the creative writing programs at the University of Oregon and Hunter College; today he is part of the Humanities Council and creative writing program at Princeton University. In the following essay, which appeared on the op-ed page of *The New York Times* in 1996, Lee remembers his mother's efforts to learn English, using literary memoir to comment on recent laws passed by certain towns in New Jersey requiring English on all commercial signs.

Before Reading

Should all commercial signs have English written on them, in addition to any other language? What about menus in ethnic restaurants?

When I read of the troubles in Palisades Park, N.J., over the proliferation 1 of Korean-language signs along its main commercial strip, I unexpectedly sympathized with the frustrations, resentments and fears of the longtime residents. They clearly felt alienated and even unwelcome in a vital part of their community. The town, like seven others in New Jersey, has passed laws requiring that half of any commercial sign in a foreign language be in English.

Now I certainly would never tolerate any exclusionary ideas about who 2 could rightfully settle and belong in the town. But having been raised in a Korean immigrant family, I saw every day the exacting price and power of language, especially with my mother, who was an outsider in an English-only world.

In the first years we lived in America, my mother could speak only the 3 most basic English, and she often encountered great difficulty whenever she went out.

We lived in New Rochelle, N.Y., in the early '70s, and most of the local 4
businesses were run by the descendants of immigrants who, generations
ago, had come to the suburbs from New York City. Proudly dotting Main
Street and North Avenue were Italian pastry and cheese shops, Jewish
tailors and cleaners and Polish and German butchers and bakers. If my
mother's marketing couldn't wait until the weekend, when my father had
free time, she would often hold off until I came home from school to buy
the groceries.

Though I was only 6 or 7 years old, she insisted that I go out shopping 5
with her and my younger sister. I mostly loathed the task, partly because
it meant I couldn't spend the afternoon playing catch with my friends but
also because I knew our errands would inevitably lead to an awkward
scene, and that I would have to speak up to help my mother.

I was just learning the language myself, but I was a quick study, as children 6
are with new tongues. I had spent kindergarten in almost complete silence,
hearing only the high nasality of my teacher and comprehending little but the
cranky wails and cries of my classmates. But soon, seemingly mere months
later, I had already become a terrible ham and mimic, and I would crack up
my father with impressions of teachers, his friends and even himself. My
mother scolded me for aping his speech, and the one time I attempted to
make light of hers I rated a roundhouse smack on my bottom.

For her, the English language was not very funny. It usually meant 7
trouble and a good dose of shame, and sometimes real hurt. Although she
had a good reading knowledge of the language from university classes in
South Korea, she had never practiced actual conversation. So in America,
she used English flashcards and phrase books and watched television with
us kids. And she faithfully carried a pocket workbook illustrated with
stick-figure people and compound sentences to be filled in.

But none of it seemed to do her much good. Staying mostly at home 8
to care for us, she didn't have many chances to try out sundry words and
phrases. When she did, say, at the window of the post office, her readied
speech would stall, freeze, sometimes altogether collapse.

One day was unusually harrowing. We ventured downtown in the 9
new Ford Country Squire my father had bought her, an enormous station
wagon that seemed as long—and deft—as an ocean liner. We were shopping for a special meal for guests visiting that weekend, and my mother had
heard that a particular butcher carried fresh oxtails—which she needed for
a traditional soup.

We'd never been inside the shop, but my mother would pause before 10
its window, which was always lined with whole hams, crown roasts and

ropes of plump handmade sausages. She greatly esteemed the bounty with her eyes, and my sister and I did also, but despite our desirous cries she'd turn us away and instead buy the packaged links at the Finast supermarket, where she felt comfortable looking them over and could easily spot the price. And, of course, not have to talk.

But that day she was resolved. The butcher store was crowded, and as 11 we stepped inside the door jingled a welcome. No one seemed to notice. We waited for some time, and people who entered after us were now being served. Finally, an old woman nudged my mother and waved a little ticket, which we hadn't taken. We patiently waited again, until one of the beefy men behind the glass display hollered our number.

My mother pulled us forward and began searching the cases, but the 12 oxtails were nowhere to be found. The man, his big arms crossed, sharply said, "Come on, lady, whaddya want?" This unnerved her, and she some-how blurted the Korean word for oxtail, soggori.

The butcher looked as if my mother had put something sour in his mouth, 13 and he glanced back at the lighted board and called the next number.

Before I knew it, she had rushed us outside and back in the wagon, 14 which she had double-parked because of the crowd. She was furious, almost vibrating with fear and grief, and I could see she was about to cry.

She wanted to go back inside, but now the driver of the car we were 15 blocking wanted to pull out. She was shooing us away. My mother, who had just earned her driver's license, started furiously working the pedals. But in her haste she must have flooded the engine, for it wouldn't turn over. The driver started honking and then another car began honking as well, and soon it seemed the entire street was shrieking at us.

In the following years, my mother grew steadily more comfortable 16 with English. In Korean, she could be fiery, stern, deeply funny and ironic; in English, just slightly less so. If she was never quite fluent, she gained enough confidence to make herself clearly known to anyone, and particu-larly to me.

Five years ago, she died of cancer, and some months after we buried 17 her I found myself in the driveway of my father's house, washing her sedan. I liked taking care of her things; it made me feel close to her. While I was cleaning out the glove compartment, I found her pocket English workbook, the one with the silly illustrations. I hadn't seen it in nearly 20 years. The yellowed pages were brittle and dog-eared. She had fash-ioned a plain-paper wrapping for it, and I wondered whether she meant to protect the book or hide it.

I don't doubt that she would have appreciated doing the family 18
shopping on the new Broad Avenue of Palisades Park. But I like to think,
too, that she would have understood those who now complain about the
Korean-only signs.

I wonder what these same people would have done if they had seen my 19
mother studying her English workbook—or lost in a store. Would they
have nodded gently at her? Would they have lent a kind word?

Thinking About the Essay

1. What is the author's purpose? Is he trying to paint a picture of his mother, describe an aspect of the immigrant experience, convey a thesis, argue a point, or what? Explain your response.

2. What is unusual about Lee's introduction? How does his position on the issue raised defy your expectations?

3. Lee offers stories within stories. How are they ordered? Which tale receives greatest development, and why?

4. Lee uses **colloquial language** in this essay. Identify some examples. What is the effect?

5. What is the dominant impression that you have of Lee's mother? How does he bring her to life?

Responding in Writing

6. Construct a profile of the writer. What do we learn about Lee? What are his values? What is his attitude toward English? How does this son of immigrant parents establish himself as an authority? How does he surprise us with his perspective on language?

7. In a personal essay, tell of a time when you were embarrassed either by the language of someone close to you or by your own use of language in a social or business situation.

8. Both Amy Tan and Chang-rae Lee focus on their mothers' handling of their second language—English. Write a comparative essay in which you explain the similarities and differences in the authors' approaches to their subject.

Networking

9. With two other class members, discuss the emotional appeal of Lee's essay. Look especially at his conclusion. Share your responses with the class.

10. Write an e-mail to your instructor, suggesting two additional questions you would ask about Lee's essay if you were teaching it.

The Power of Words in Wartime

ROBIN TOLMACH LAKOFF

Robin Tolmach Lakoff was born in Brooklyn, New York, in 1942 and educated at Radcliffe College (B.A., 1964), Indiana University (M.A., 1965), and Harvard University (Ph.D., 1967). An influential linguist who serves on the faculty at the University of California at Berkeley, Lakoff has written several studies focusing on the influence of language on social attitudes—especially attitudes toward women and "others." Among her most important works are *Language and Women's Place* (1975), *Talking Power: The Politics of Language in Our Lives* (1990), and *The Language of War* (2000). The following essay appeared in the *The New York Times* on May 18, 2004.

Before Reading

What does "stereotyping" mean? What is the relationship between stereotyping and such words in wartime as "terrorist," "jihadist," "invader," "infidel"?

An American soldier refers to an Iraqi prisoner as "it." A general speaks not of "Iraqi fighters" but of "the enemy." A weapons manufacturer doesn't talk about people but about ''targets." 1

Bullets and bombs are not the only tools of war. Words, too, play their part. 2

Human beings are social animals, genetically hard-wired to feel compassion toward others. Under normal conditions, most people find it very difficult to kill. 3

But in war, military recruits must be persuaded that killing other people is not only acceptable but even honorable. 4

The language of war is intended to bring about that change, and not only for soldiers in the field. In wartime, language must be created to enable combatants and noncombatants alike to see the other side as killable, to overcome the innate queasiness over the taking of human life. Soldiers, and those who remain at home, learn to call their enemies by names that make them seem not quite human—inferior, contemptible and not like "us." 5

The specific words change from culture to culture and war to war. The names need not be obviously demeaning. Just the fact that we can name them gives us a sense of superiority and control. If, in addition, we give them 6 nicknames, we can see them as smaller, weaker and childlike—not worth taking seriously as fully human.

The Greeks and Romans referred to everyone else as "barbarians"— 7 etymologically those who only babble, only go "bar-bar." During the American Revolution, the British called the colonists "Yankees," a term with a history that is still in dispute. While the British intended it disparagingly, the Americans, in perhaps the first historical instance of reclamation, made the word their own and gave it a positive spin, turning the derisive song "Yankee Doodle" into our first, if unofficial, national anthem.

In World War I, the British gave the Germans the nickname "Jerries," 8 from the first syllable of German. In World War II, Americans referred to the Japanese as "Japs."

The names may refer to real or imagined cultural and physical dif- 9 ferences that emphasize the ridiculous or the repugnant. So in various wars, the British called the French "Frogs." Germans have been called "Krauts," a reference to weird and smelly food. The Vietnamese were called "slopes" and "slants." The Koreans were referred to simply as "gooks."

The war in Iraq has added new examples. Some American soldiers refer 10 to the Iraqis as "hadjis," used in a derogatory way, apparently unaware that the word, which comes from the Arabic term for a pilgrimage to Mecca, is used as a term of respect for older Muslim men.

The Austrian ethologist Konrad Lorenz suggested that the more clearly 11 we see other members of our own species as individuals, the harder we find it to kill them.

So some terms of war are collective nouns, encouraging us to see the 12 enemy as an undifferentiated mass, rather than as individuals capable of suffering. Crusaders called their enemy "the Saracen," and in World War I, the British called Germans "the Hun."

American soldiers are trained to call those they are fighting against "the 13 enemy." It is easier to kill an enemy than an Iraqi.

The word "enemy" itself provides the facelessness of a collective noun. 14 Its non-specificity also has a fear-inducing connotation; enemy means simply "those we are fighting," without reference to their identity.

The terrors and uncertainties of war make learning this kind of lan- 15 guage especially compelling for soldiers on the front. But civilians back home also need to believe that what their country is doing is just and necessary, and that the killing they are supporting is in some way different from the killing in civilian life that is rightly punished by the criminal justice system. The use of the language developed for military purposes by civilians reassures them that war is not murder.

The linguistic habits that soldiers must absorb in order to fight make 16 atrocities like those at Abu Ghraib virtually inevitable. The same language that creates a psychological chasm between ''us'' and ''them'' and enables American troops to kill in battle, makes enemy soldiers fit subjects for torture and humiliation. The reasoning is: They are not really human, so they will not feel the pain.

Once language draws that line, all kinds of mistreatment become imag- 17 inable, and then justifiable. To make the abuses at Abu Ghraib unthinkable, we would have to abolish war itself.

Thinking About the Essay

1. Lakoff wrote this essay as an op-ed article for a newspaper. What aspects of style, thesis placement, paragraph organization, length, and tone does she employ to satisfy the demands of an op-ed contribution?

2. What is Lakoff's purpose in this essay? Does she want to inform readers about language, analyze words in wartime, argue about the Iraq war, or what?

3. Lakoff organizes her essay around causes and effects, using a series of examples to support her causal analysis. Trace this strategy through the essay, trying to determine where language is a cause, an effect, or both.

4. How logical do you find Lakoff's article, and why? Do you think that she succumbs to any logical fallacies or exaggerates in order to make a point? Justify your response.

5. How effective do you find Lakoff's attempt to link the language stemming from the war in Iraq with that of the language used to invoke the "enemy" in wars stretching back in history to ancient Greece? Is this sufficient support for her thesis or claim? Explain.

Responding in Writing

6. Select one word that appears prominently in discussions of the war in Iraq (or Afghanistan, or both), and demonstrate the ways in which government and the press invoke this word to influence public attitudes.

7. Write a cause-and-effect essay in which you demonstrate the ways in which language can stereotype certain types of people—for example, immigrants, Muslims, gays, Africans.

8. Argue for or against the proposition that Lakoff presents a convincing argument in "The Power of Words in Wartime." Refer to specific strategies she employs to support your position.

Networking

9. Lakoff refers to Konrad Lorenz in paragraph 11. With one other class member, go online and find out more about this person. Then explain in class discussion why you think Lakoff refers to him in her essay.

10. Go online to find out more about Abu Ghraib, a topic that Lakoff injects into her essay. Download at least three images of this episode, and then write a brief essay, with illustrations, highlighting Lakoff's claim about the "psychological chasm between 'us' and 'them.'"

Lingua Franchise

CHARLES FORAN | Charles Foran is from Toronto and holds degrees from the University of Toronto and University College, Dublin. He has taught at universities in China, Hong Kong, and Canada. Foran is the author of eight books, including four novels, and writes regularly for Canadian journals. He has also produced radio documentaries for the Canadian Broadcasting Company's *Ideas* program on subjects ranging from Hong Kong Cinema to contemporary Indian writing. In the following piece, which first appeared in *The Walrus Magazine* in November 2004, Foran looks at how English has been adopted and adapted in the global marketplace.

Before Reading

What elements of a slang dialect make an appearance in your casual speech? How many people do you know who practice this dialect?

In a restaurant in Singapore's Little India district I chatted recently with a man doling out bowls of fish-head curry. He called me a *"mat saleh,"* Malay for 'white foreigner.' He also dubbed a woman who walked past us an "S.P.G."—a 'Sarong Party Girl.' According to him, upper-crust Singaporians who put on posh accents were "chiak kantang." "Chiak" is Hokkien for 'eating,' "kantang" a mangling of the Malay for 'potatoes.' 'Eating potatoes': affecting Western mannerisms.

Singapore has four official languages: Mandarin, English, Malay, and Tamil. At street level, however, there is no mother tongue. Except for among older Chinese, who still speak the Hokkien dialect, the city-state's lingua franca is actually Singlish, a much-loved, much-frowned-upon hodge-podge of languages and slang. When the man in the restaurant asked if I could pay with a smaller bill, he expressed it this way: "Got, lah?" I recognized that bit of cobbling. In Hong Kong, where I was then living, Cantonese speakers sprinkle their English with similar punctuation. 'Lah' often denotes a question, like 'eh' for Canadians. 'Wah' infers astonishment. Once, when I was walking through that city's nightclub district with a Chinese friend, we nearly knocked into a Canto-pop star, a young man of smoldering Elvis looks. "Wah, now can die!" my friend said, only half-jokingly.

If English is the region's compromise tongue, default neutral terrain for 3 doing deals and making friends, loan words and hybrid street dialects serve to advance its utility. It is the same across most of Asia. In the Philippines, Tagalog speakers refer to a look-alike as a "Xerox" and an out-dated fad as a "chapter." "Golets," they say, meaning 'Let's go.' Anything first-rate in Bombay gets called "cheese," from 'chiz,' the Hindi word for 'object.' In Japan, students on a Friday night announce "Let's beer!" and salarymen quit smoking because of a "dokuto-sutoppu" a 'doctor-stop,' or orders from their physician. The majority of these word constructions would be no more comprehensible to a North American than the latest slang out of England or Australia. They belong to the places that formed them.

All this activity marks an interesting point from which to examine the 4 latest evidence surrounding the explosion of English, which now boasts 1.9 billion competent speakers worldwide. In the view of Montreal writer Mark Abley, author of *Spoken Here: Travels Among Threatened Languages*, "no other language has ever enjoyed the political, economic, cultural, and military power that now accompanies English." English, he says, acts like a "brand name" and serves as a "repository of global ambition." Describing a quiz given to young Malaysians that contained references to American culture, Abley reports: "The obvious theme is the United States. But the subtler theme, I think, is power."

"Language annihilation," he writes, may just be one battle in the 5 "wider war"—"the fight to sustain diversity on a planet where globalizing, assimilating, and eradicating occur on a massive scale." Mark Abley is far from alone in linking the spread of English with fears of a bland consumerist empire—i.e. with a certain vision of American might. Geoffrey Hull, an Australian linguist quoted in *Spoken Here,* advises the banning of unsubtitled English programming on TV in East Timor. "English," Hull warns, "is a killer language."

Such unease isn't hard to understand. Of the 6,000 living languages, 6 some 90 percent are at risk of vanishing before the end of this century. These are tongues spoken by fewer than 100, 000 people, and rarely as the only means of communication. For some linguists, the death of each marks the disappearance of a world view. Without a language to call one's own, original stories stop being told and unique conversations with God diminish. English triumphs just one set of stories and one conversation.

But is the link between the "tidal wave" of English, as Abley describes   7
it, and the threat to variety so direct? History isn't without precedents for this kind of upheaval. With a few centuries of the empire in Ancient Greece, for instance, languages spoken by Trojans, Sumerians, Lydians, Etruscans and Scythians, to name a few, had been rendered extinct. Each of those societies contributed to the first great renaissance in western civilization. Classical Greek itself went on to serve as a foundation for a few other languages, including this one.

Cries of English the cultural barbarian aren't new, either. In the 19th   8
century, France's *civilisatrice* and Germany's *kultur* programs granted the colonial aggressions of those nations a patina of benevolence. England's ambitions, in contrast, were given no similar benefit of the doubt, being equated from the start with an unbridled lust for power. Over the past fifty years, as the U.S. has come to supplant Cruel Britannia as the primary 'exporter' of the tongue, it has come to bear most of the criticisms. When a Muslim group recently denounced the Arabic version of the *Idol* TV series because it "facilitates the culture of globalization led by America," it didn't matter that the program had originated in England. In certain minds, English can only ever be the language of McDonald's and Nike, Madonna and Cruise.

By this reasoning, English couldn't form a natural part of Singaporian   9
street life or Filipino cross-language talk. It couldn't be the rightful possession of the millions of Indians who now call it their mother tongue. But the truth is, English isn't just exploding across the universe; it is being exploded on contact with other societies and languages. No single political power or region, it could be argued, can fairly claim it as its exclusive spokesperson.

In Asia, at least, English certainly feels this protean. The Hong Kong   10
author Nury Vittachi has been charting the emergence of a pan-Southeast-Asian argot. He calls the argot 'Englasian,' the wonky dialect of international business types and youthful hipsters. Vittachi even penned a short play in Englasian called *Don't Stupid Lah, Brudder*. The setting is a bar in a Jakarta hotel and the characters are a Malaysian investor, an Indian accountant, and an Australian entrepreneur. The Malay says things like "No nid-lah, sit-sit, don't shy." The Auzzie counters with "Don't do yer lolly, mate. Let's have a squiz." Of the three, the Indian is the most readily intelligible. She speaks of how she might be able to "facilitate my cousin-brother, a revered Sydneysider."

Spend any time in the region and two things become obvious. First, 11 English still makes only a minor noise, and only in the major cities. Its consumer blandishments pale against home-grown magazines, movies, and pop singers. No major Asian language, be it Mandarin, Malay, Japanese, or any of the fourteen principal Indian tongues, is at risk of vanishing. Interestingly, those languages are themselves killing off their own sub-dialects and non-standard variants. The world is everywhere too connected for the health of the linguistically vulnerable.

The second observation relates to the playfulness of inventions like 12 Singlish. If Asians are threatened by the growing presence of English, they are expressing their fear in the strangest manner—by inviting the danger into their homes. Linguists praise a language for its capacity to acquire and assimilate expressions from elsewhere. Such openness is taken as a sign of confidence and growth. The principal languages of nearly half of humanity are, by this measure, prospering. English isn't storming these cultures to wage war on them. The locals, at least, aren't under that impression. They view the language mostly as a tool, one they can manipulate, and even make their own.

Thinking About the Essay

1. What is the pun in the title? Is this, in your opinion, an appropriate title for the essay?

2. What is the effect of the rapid translations of phrases and terms given in the first two paragraphs? How important is the narrator's identity or point of view?

3. According to the author, how do languages work at the "street level," in contrast to the "official" level? In what sense do loan words and hybrid street dialects "advance [the] utility" of English (paragraph 3)?

4. What is the author's attitude toward the critic Geoffrey Hull and his conclusion that English is a "killer language" (paragraph 5)?

5. What does Foran mean when he writes (in paragraph 11) that the "world is everywhere too connected for the health of the linguistically vulnerable"?

Responding in Writing

6. Is it true that the death of a language "marks the disappearance of a world view" (paragraph 6)? In a brief essay, consider the relationship between language and thought. How can language *give birth* to a worldview?

7. Do you agree with Foran's claim that "no single political power or region ... can fairly claim [English] as its exclusive spokesperson" (paragraph 9)? Respond to this statement in an argumentative essay.

8. Compare Foran's critique of those who view language as an instrument of commercial exploitation with Robin Lakoff's argument in "The Power of Words in Wartime." Where do these writers' positions converge and where do they diverge?

Networking

9. As a class, make a list of words or phrases that have been recently acquired and assimilated in American English. Is it accurate to say of any of these new acquisitions that they also introduce a new set of *concepts*?

10. Go online and perform a Google search of one of the terms or phrases Foran heard in the Singapore restaurant (paragraphs 1–2). How does this language appear in print, online, in contrast to the spoken context Foran describes?

Multilingual America

WILLIAM H. FREY

William H. Frey is a senior fellow of demographic studies at the Metropolitan Policy Program at the Brookings Institution in Washington, DC. He is also on the faculty of the Population Studies Center at the University of Michigan. In the following essay, which appeared in the July/August 2002 issue of *American Demographics,* Frey analyzes the rise in American households where the inhabitants speak a language other than English. The writer offers data drawn from the 2000 United States Census to trace recent population shifts, the rise of ethnic communities in urban and nonurban areas, and the impact on the American "melting pot" of people who speak a language other than English at home.

Before Reading

How can English be taught to new immigrants who stay in their own ethnic communities and prefer to speak their own language at home? If you were involved in policymaking, what programs would you design for these individuals?

America's identity as a melting pot now extends beyond multiple races   1
and cultures to also include numerous languages. Ours is an increasingly multilingual nation, due to a new wave of immigration.

The number of individuals who speak a language other than English at   2
home is on the rise. This population is also on the move: No longer restricted to traditional port-of-entry cities, such as New York and Los Angeles,

foreign-language speakers are now sprouting up in certain Southeastern and Western states.

For the first time, thanks to Census 2000 long-form data, we are able to identify these new locations where residents who speak a foreign language are making their presence felt. Although relatively small, this population is beginning to constitute a critical mass in many communities—reason alone for businesses seeking new markets to take note. 3

Nationally, Americans age 5 and older who speak a language other than English at home grew 47 percent in the past decade. According to Census 2000, this group now accounts for slightly less than 1 in 5 Americans (17.9 percent). About three-fifths of this group speak Spanish at home (59.9 percent), another fifth speaks another Indo-European language (21.3 percent) and almost 15 percent speak an Asian language. 4

Overall, foreign-language speakers grew by about 15 million during the 1990s, with new Spanish speakers contributing about 11 million people and new Asian speakers almost 2.5 million. Continued immigration from Latin America and Asia has increased the number of people who speak languages native to those regions. 5

Foreign-Language Havens

These foreign-language speakers are concentrated in 10 states, each where 20 percent or more of the residents speak a language other than English at home. Led by California (40 percent), this group includes several other Western states as well as New York, New Jersey, Florida and Rhode Island. The concentration is even more evident when one looks at individual metropolitan areas. (See Table 4.1.) 6

In six metros, including Miami and Laredo, Texas, those who speak only English at home are in the minority. In five Mexican border towns in this category, Spanish accounts for more than 96 percent of non-English languages spoken. 7

Other areas where more than one-third of the population speaks a language other than English at home include Los Angeles, San Antonio, San Francisco, New York and San Diego. 8

By far, the two largest metros that house the most foreign-language-speakers are Los Angeles and New York, with more than 7 million and 6 million foreign-language speakers, respectively. Together, these two gateways increased their foreign-language-speaking populations by 3.5 million between 1990 and 2000, accounting for 24 percent of the country's total gain. (See Figure 4.1.) 9

Eight metropolitan areas with the largest populations that speak a foreign language accounted for almost half (46 percent) of the nation's total gain. 10

Others include Phoenix, Atlanta, Las Vegas, Seattle and Denver—cities that became secondary magnets for new immigrant groups during the 1990s.

Multilingual Expansion

Although many immigrant gateway metros still hold the lion's share 11 of inhabitants who speak a foreign language, the 1990s was a decade of extensive redistribution of foreign-born residents and hence, of

TABLE 4.1 Spanish and Asian Language Magnets

There is some overlap between the lists of communities forming new, fast-growing enclaves of speakers of Spanish and Asian languages. The areas below all have at least 5,000 Spanish-speaking or Asian-speaking residents.

Persons speaking Spanish at home: Metro areas with greatest growth, 1990–2000	% Increase 1990–2000
Fayetteville-Springdale-Rogers, AR MSA*	609%
Elkhart-Goshen, IN MSA	403%
Raleigh-Durham–Chapel Hill, NC MSA	381%
Charlotte-Gastonia–Rock Hill, NC-SC MSA	376%
Greensboro-Winston-Salem–High Point, NC MSA	367%
Green Bay, WI MSA	354%
Hickory-Morganton-Lenoir, NC MSA	338%
Atlanta, GA MSA	314%
Fort Smith, AR-OK MSA	310%
Sioux City, IA-NE MSA	306%
Persons speaking Asian language at home: Metro areas with greatest growth, 1990–2000	
Hickory-Morganton-Lenoir, NC MSA	467%
Las Vegas, NV-AZ MSA	220%
Charlotte-Gastonia–Rock Hill, NC-SC MSA	182%
Lincoln, NE MSA	172%
Greenville-Spartanburg-Anderson, SC MSA	170%
Atlanta, GA MSA	157%
Greensboro-Winston-Salem–High Point, NC MSA	156%
Austin-San Marcos, TX MSA	156%
Raleigh-Durham–Chapel Hill, NC MSA	128%
Grand Rapids-Muskegon-Holland, MI MSA	127%

Source: William H. Frey analysis, 1990 and 2000 U.S. Census.

*MSA = Metropolitan Statistical Area as defined by the Office of Management and Budget.

FIGURE 4.1 Native Tongues

Ten states have the largest shares of foreign-language speakers (more than one in five speaks a foreign language at home). These include several Western states, New York, New Jersey, Florida, and Rhode Island.

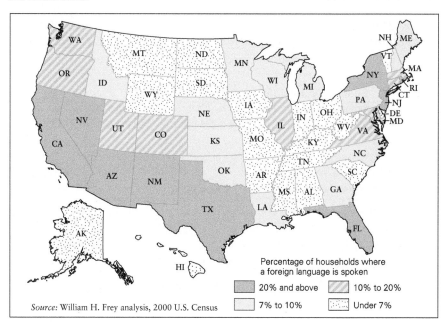

Source: William H. Frey analysis, 2000 U.S. Census

Percentage of households where a foreign language is spoken

- 20% and above
- 10% to 20%
- 7% to 10%
- Under 7%

foreign-language speakers. Areas that had little prior familiarity with Spanish-speaking residents or those who speak an Asian language gained exposure to cultural as well as linguistic differences in their communities.

States that now have the fastest growing non-English-speaking populations are not typically those with the highest percentages of such people. (See Figure 4.2.) Most are Southeastern and Western states that began to attract new immigrants, often in response to an increased demand for services due to an influx of migrants from other states. 12

In the Southeast, this includes Georgia, North Carolina, Arkansas, Tennessee and Virginia; in the West, Arizona, Nevada, Utah, Oregon, Washington, Idaho and Colorado. Several interior states with small foreign-born populations, such as Nebraska, are also attracting new non-English-speaking residents to take a variety of service jobs. 13

Similar geographic patterns are evident in metropolitan areas with the fastest growth of foreign-language speakers. For example, Fayetteville, Ark., increased its non-English-speaking population by a whopping 368 14

FIGURE 4.2 Foreign-Language Growth, 1990–2000

The states with the fastest-growing non-English-speaking populations are not typically those with the highest percentages of foreign-language speakers. Such states include Georgia and North Carolina as well as Nebraska and Washington.

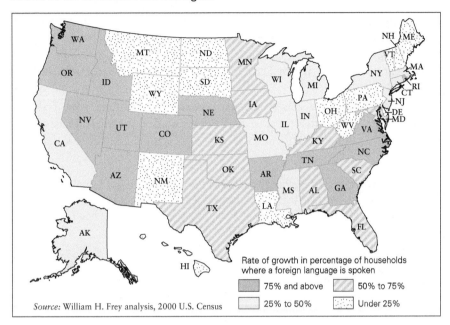

Rate of growth in percentage of households where a foreign language is spoken

75% and above | 50% to 75%
25% to 50% | Under 25%

Source: William H. Frey analysis, 2000 U.S. Census

percent during the 1990s. Six of the seven fastest-growing areas (Las Vegas being the exception) are in the South, including the North Carolina metros of Hickory, Raleigh-Durham–Chapel Hill, Charlotte and Greensboro.

Although in many of these enclaves foreign-language speakers account 15 for only a small percentage of the area's total population, this is not the case for all. Las Vegas, for example, increased its share of residents who speak a foreign language to 24 percent, from 13 percent, between 1990 and 2000. Similar increases can be seen for Orlando and Naples, Fla.; Phoenix and Dallas. Significant gains also occurred in small Iowa cities, such as Sioux City, Waterloo and Des Moines.

Spanish and Asian Language Magnets

While Spanish dominates the foreign languages spoken at home on the 16 national level, this is not true for all parts of the United States. For example, fewer than half the foreign-language speakers in San Francisco and New York City speak Spanish. In the former, nearly as many speak Asian languages; in the latter, a large number of residents continue to speak other European languages at home.

Spanish represents more than half the foreign languages spoken at 17 home in only nine states. These are located mostly on the Mexican border and in the West. Metro areas with the largest Spanish-speaking shares of their populations reflect the same geographic pattern.

In contrast, metropolitan areas that house large shares of Asian popula- 18 tions are fewer and farther between. Honolulu tops the group, with Asian languages spoken by almost 9 out of 10 people who speak a non-English language at home, followed by San Francisco, Los Angeles, San Diego and Stockton, Calif.

Considerable overlap exists between communities forming new, fast- 19 growing enclaves for Spanish speakers and those who speak an Asian language. (See Tables 4.2 and 4.3.) Of the 15 metro areas with the fastest-growing

TABLE 4.2   Metros with Highest Shares of Foreign-Language Speakers, 2000
Six metros, including Laredo and Miami, have populations where the minority speak only English at home. In five Mexican border towns in this category, Spanish is the non-English language spoken in more than 96 percent of homes.

Name	Percent speaking non-English languages at home	Percent who speak these languages at home			
		Spanish	Asian language	European language	Other
Laredo, TX MSA	91.9%	99.4%	0.3%	0.3%	0.0%
McAllen-Edinburg-Mission, TX MSA	83.1%	99.0%	0.5%	0.4%	0.0%
Brownsville-Harlingen–San Benito, TX MSA	79.0%	99.1%	0.4%	0.4%	0.1%
El Paso, TX MSA	73.3%	97.1%	1.0%	1.6%	0.3%
Las Cruces, NM MSA	54.4%	96.7%	0.7%	1.9%	0.7%
Miami–Fort Lauderdale, FL CMSA	51.5%	80.0%	1.9%	16.7%	1.4%
Salinas, CA MSA	47.3%	83.5%	9.1%	6.5%	0.9%
Los Angeles–Riverside–Orange County, CA CMSA	46.8%	70.7%	18.2%	9.1%	1.9%
Yuma, AZ MSA	45.5%	95.6%	1.5%	1.9%	0.9%
Merced, CA MSA	45.2%	77.7%	11.6%	10.4%	0.4%

Source: William H. Frey analysis, 2000 U.S. Census.

TABLE 4.3 Metros with Largest Number of Foreign-Language Speakers, 2000
The two largest metros with foreign-language speakers are Los Angeles and New York. Together they increased their foreign-language-speaking population by 3.5 million during the 1990s—about 24 percent of the nation's total gain.

Largest number of foreign-language speakers, 2000	*Number of people*
Los Angeles–Riverside–Orange County, CA CMSA	7, 080.474
New York–Northern New Jersey–Long Island, NY-NJ-CT-PA CMSA	6, 614.354
San Francisco–Oakland–San Jose, CA CMSA	2, 368.377
Chicago-Gary-Kenosha, IL-IN-WI CMSA	2, 116.043
Miami–Fort Lauderdale, FL CMSA	1, 869.966
Houston-Galveston-Brazoria, TX CMSA	1, 372.010
Dallas–Fort Worth, TX CMSA	1, 163.502
Washington-Baltimore, DC-MD-VA-WV CMSA	1, 158.677
Boston-Worcester-Lawrence, MA-NH-ME-CT CMSA	1, 042.727

Source: William H. Frey analysis, 1990 and 2000 U.S. Census.

Spanish-speaking populations, six are on the list of fast-growing, Asian-language-speaking areas. These include Atlanta and Las Vegas, as well as North Carolina metros Raleigh-Durham, Charlotte, Greensboro and Hickory.

These areas are attracting new residents as a result of local universities 20 or the labor market pulls associated with general population growth and the fast-growing economies of the "New Sun Belt."

English Proficiency

One issue raised when people who speak a foreign language become new 21 residents of a community is how well they can conduct their lives in English. While it's no surprise that immigrants who have lived in the U.S. for a long time become fluent in English, Census 2000 reveals that this may not be the case with new arrivals.

The Census Bureau asked people who speak a language other than 22 English at home this question: How well does this person speak English? (The choices were: very well, well, not well or not at all.) Between 1990 and 2000, there was a larger increase of Spanish speakers who could not speak English very well than of those who could. However, for Asian language speakers, there was a larger increase between 1990 and 2000 of those who could speak English very well.

To a great extent, Spanish speakers arriving in non-gateway areas are 23 less likely to speak English very well. Among the metros with the lowest percentages of Spanish speakers speaking English very well are Greensboro, Raleigh-Durham, Charlotte and Hickory in North Carolina; Atlanta and other newer destinations for Spanish-speaking residents.

Among areas where Spanish speakers have high levels of English pro- 24 ficiency are university towns like Gainesville, Fla., and Lubbock, Texas, as well as locales with long-standing Spanish-speaking residents, such as Albuquerque, N.M.

The same pattern occurs among residents who speak an Asian language, 25 with lower levels of proficiency where such settlers are relatively new (e.g., Lincoln, Neb.; Grand Rapids, Mich.; Minneapolis–St. Paul, Minn.; Greensboro, N.C. and Atlanta). High levels of proficiency tend to be in university communities such as Gainesville, Fla.; Raleigh-Durham and Chapel Hill, N.C.; Champagne-Urbana, Ill. and Colorado Springs, Colo.

These patterns of English proficiency mirror the national picture. 26 States with the lowest levels of English proficiency tend to be those that had the fastest growth of foreign-language residents during the 1990s. Nebraska, Nevada, Oregon, North Carolina and Georgia are part of this group of states, which also includes some longer-term havens for foreign-born and foreign-language-speaking residents. For example, less than half (49 percent) of California's foreign-born residents speak English very well.

The new census data provides insights into this fast growing group of 27 Americans who speak a language other than English at home. It also highlights the fact that if the U.S. is to continue to live up to its reputation as a melting pot, this influx of foreign-language speakers will require special efforts on the parts of schools, local organizations and grassroots groups to enable these new residents to become fully integrated members of their communities.

Thinking About the Essay

1. How would you describe the writer's audience for this essay? What assumptions does he make about this audience? How does he mold his style to the expectations of the audience?

2. Explain the significance of the writer's title. What approach does he take to his subject? In other words, what is his purpose? How does his purpose govern his thesis?

3. Where is the thesis stated? How does the conclusion reinforce the thesis or color it with a mildly argumentative edge?

4. Frey employs a considerable amount of data in this essay. How relevant are these data? What aspects of the data do you find interesting? What aspects, if any, do you find weak or irrelevant? There are several visual illustrations in this essay. What types of data do they present? How do you "read" them in terms of their significance? What do they contribute to the article?

5. The author divides his essay into sections. Summarize each section. How does each section flow from the previous unit? Is the author able to achieve unity and coherence? Justify your response.

Responding in Writing

6. Use the data provided by Frey to write your own essay entitled "Our Shrinking Language Tapestry." Make your essay more argumentative than Frey's. Take a stand on the demographics Frey provides, and back up your claim with at least three good reasons or minor propositions.

7. If you belong to a family in which members normally speak a language other than English, tell about their attitude toward the use of English. Or imagine that you are part of such a household. What would your perception of your native language and this second language— English—be?

8. In the last paragraphs, Frey implies that it is important to learn English to become "fully integrated" into one's community. In an argumentative essay, agree or disagree with his statement.

Networking

9. In groups of four, obtain a copy of the 2000 United States Census, and focus on the data about immigration patterns and language use that this document provides. Then construct a group report of approximately 1,000 words highlighting and interpreting this data.

10. Go to one or more search engines and type in "English only" or "English Only Movement." Try other combinations if necessary. Download relevant information, and then participate in a class discussion of this controversy.

Reading the History of the World

ISABEL ALLENDE | Isabel Allende, the daughter of a Chilean diplomat, was born in 1942 in Lima, Peru. Isabel moved from Peru to Chile, where she was living and working at the time her uncle, Salvador Allende, the president of Chile, was assassinated during an army coup, assisted by the CIA, in 1973. "In that moment," she says, "I realized that everything was possible—that violence was a dimension that was always around you." The Allende family did not think that the new regime would last, and Isabel Allende continued to work as a noted journalist. However, when it became too dangerous to remain in Chile, the family went into exile in Venezuela. Allende's first novel, *The House of the Spirits* (1985), established her as a significant writer in the tradition of "magic realism" associated with the Nobel Prize winner Gabriel García Márquez. Other novels include *Of Love and Shadows* (1987), *Eva Luna* (1988), *Daughter of Fortune* (1999), and *Zorro* (2005). Allende has also written two memoirs, *Paula* (1995) and *The Sum of Our Days* (2007) as well as stories for children. Allende has spoken of the "wind of exile" that makes it necessary to recover memories of one's native land. In this essay, which appears in a collection of essays on reading by well-known writers, *Speaking of Reading* (1995), she invokes the act of reading as one way to salvage these memories.

Before Reading

Allende declares that only through reading can we fully become aware of "injustice and misery and violence." Would you agree or disagree, and why?

Reading is like looking through several windows which open to an infinite landscape. I abandon myself to the pleasure of the journey. How could I know about other people, how could I know about the history of the world, how could my mind expand and grow if I could not read? I began to read when I was very small; I learned to read and write practically when I was a baby. For me, life without reading would be like being in prison, it would be as if my spirit were in a straitjacket; life would be a very dark and narrow place. 1

I was brought up in a house full of books. It was a big, strange, somber house, the house of my grandparents. My uncle, who lived in the house, had a lot of books—he collected them like holy relics. His room held a ton of books. Few newspapers were allowed in that house because my grandfather was a very patriarchal, conservative man who thought that newspapers, as well as the radio, were full of vulgar ideas (at that time we didn't have TV), so the only contact I had with the world, really, was through my uncle's books. No one censored or guided my reading; I read anything I wanted. 2

Isabel Allende "Reading the History of the World." Excerpt from Isabel Allende from *Speaking of Reading*, edited by Nadine Rosenthal. Copyright © 1995. Reprinted by permission of Nadine Rosenthal.

I began reading Shakespeare when I was nine, not because of the 3
language or the beauty, but because of the plot and the great characters. I
have always been interested in adventure, plot, strong characters, history,
animals. As a child, I read children's books, most of the Russian literature,
many French authors, and later, Latin American writers. I think I belong
to the first generation of writers in Latin America who were brought up
reading Latin American literature; earlier generations read European and
North American literature. Our books were very badly distributed.

Books allow me to see my feelings put into words. After I read the femi- 4
nist authors from North America, I could finally find words for the anger
that I had all my life. I was brought up in a male chauvinist society and I
had accumulated much anger, yet I couldn't express it. I could only be angry
and do crazy things, but I couldn't put my anger into words and use it in a
rational, articulate way. After I read those books, things became clearer to
me, I could talk about that anger and express it in a more positive way.

The same thing happened with politics. I was aware of injustice and mis- 5
ery and political violence, but I couldn't express my feelings until I read about
those issues and realized that other people had been dealing with them for
centuries, and had already invented the words to express what I was feeling.

I have often been separated from my mother, whom I love very much. 6
She now lives in Chile and we write a letter to each other every day. We
talk about what we've read or what we are writing. I do it the first thing
every morning of my life, even when I'm traveling. It's as if I were writing
a journal. It's like having a long conversation with her; we are connected
with a strong bond. This same bond also connects me with my daughter,
who is living in Spain, because when I write the letter to my mother, I make
a copy that goes to my daughter, and they do the same. This is becoming a
very strange network of letters.

My mother is a much better reader than I. My reading is very fast, hectic, 7
disorganized, and impatient. If I'm not caught in the first pages I abandon
the book. My mother, however, is very patient and goes very slowly. She is
the only person who reads my manuscripts, helping me to edit, revise, and
correct them. She has a strong sense of poetry and such good taste. She's very
well informed, very cultivated, very sensitive, and loves reading.

I have tried to give my children the love of books. My daughter is a good 8
reader. She's a psychologist and has to read a lot of professional books, but
she loves novels, short stories, poetry. My son, however, doesn't read any
fiction. He's a scientific person with a mathematical mentality. I've tried to
imagine how his mind and heart work, without nourishment from books,
but I can't. He's a great boy, but how can he do it? I don't know.

My uncle, Salvador Allende, who was President of Chile before he was 9 assassinated during the military coup, hardly affected my life. I liked him and loved him, but only as I do other relatives. He was the best man at my wedding. I was never involved in politics, and never participated in his government. (I became interested in politics only after the coup.) He was not a very strong reader of fiction, actually. He was always reading reports, essays, books about politics, sociology, economy, etc. He was a very well-informed person and he read very fast, his eyes practically skimming across the page to get the necessary information, but when he wanted to relax, he would rather watch a movie than read.

During the three years of Allende's government, any Chilean could buy 10 books of "Quimantu," the state publishing house, for very little money, the equivalent of two newspapers. In this way he hoped to promote culture. His goal was that every single Chilean could read and write and be able to buy as many books as he or she wanted by the end of his term.

My own experience of life, my biography, my feelings, my self as a per- 11 son, affect my reading. The writer puts out half of the book, but then I read the book in my own unique manner. This is why reading is so interesting; we as readers don't have passive roles, but very active ones. We must integrate into the text our own experiences of life and our own feelings. While reading a book, we are constantly applying our own knowledge.

Our backgrounds determine our strengths and interests as readers. Many 12 themes that are extremely popular in North America are impossible for me to read because they aren't part of my culture—I just don't care about them. For example, I can't relate to those books by daughters who write against their mothers. But if I read a book by Toni Morrison or Louise Erdrich that deals with being a woman and part of an ethnic minority, I can relate to its content. Also, I like Latin American authors very much, especially Jorge Amado, García Márquez, Mario Vargas Llosa, Juan Rulfo, Jorge Luis Borges, and many others. There are a few Latin American women writers that I enjoy as well, but they have been badly distributed and poorly reviewed. Latin American literature has been an exclusively male club, to say the least.

I have met many people, including well-informed, educated people, 13 who actually take pride in the fact that they haven't read anything by a woman. Recently, I received a clipping from a newspaper in Chile. It was a public letter to me from a Chilean entertainer apologizing that he had never before read any of my books because I am a woman. He wrote that he never read literature written by women. After he made a special effort to read my books, he felt he must apologize to me and say that I could actually write.

I will always be interested in programs of illiteracy because it is such a 14
common problem in my continent: 50 percent of the population of Latin
America cannot read or write, and of those who can, only a few can afford
books or have the habit of reading. To me, not reading is like having the
spirit imprisoned.

Thinking About the Essay

1. List the images, metaphors, and **similes** that Allende presents in her
   introductory paragraph. What is her purpose? What is the effect?

2. State Allende's thesis. Is it stated or implied? Explain.

3. What strategies does Allende employ to blend personal experience and
   analysis? What, specifically, is she analyzing, and how does she develop
   her topics?

4. Allende devotes two paragraphs to her uncle, Salvador Allende (paragraphs
   9 and 10). Why? How do these paragraphs influence the tone of the entire
   essay?

5. What causal connections does Allende establish between the acts of
   reading and writing and the state of society in Latin America?

Responding in Writing

6. Write an essay in which you describe your reading habits as a child and as
   an adult. Did you live in a house filled with books? Did you enjoy reading?
   What were your favorite books? Who were the readers and nonreaders in
   your family? Answer these questions in a personal essay.

7. Allende refers to the fact that half of the population in Latin America is
   illiterate. Write an analytical essay that examines the impact of illiteracy on
   a society or nation.

8. Imagine a reading plan for your children, and write about it. Will you leave
   reading development exclusively to teachers? How will you regulate your
   child's reading and television viewing habits? Do you agree with Allende
   that reading can open children to "an infinite landscape" (paragraph 1)?

Networking

9. Discuss in small groups the nature of your reading habits during various
   stages in your life. Report to the class on your discoveries.

10. Find out more about Salvador Allende and the Allende family. Search the
    Internet or conduct an advanced search with the assistance of a college
    librarian. Try to find specific information on Allende's literacy crusade.

Chapter 8: Speaking in Tongues: Does Language Unify or Divide Us?

SHARON BEGLEY

Sharon Begley (1956–), a graduate of Yale University, has pursued a career in journalism reporting on neuroscience, genetics, physics, astronomy, anthropology, and cognitive science for Newsweek, *the* Wall Street Journal, The Daily Beast, *and* Reuters. *She is the author of* Train Your Mind, Change Your Brain *(2007) and the co-author of* The Mind and the Brain *(with Jeffrey Schwartz, 2002) and* The Emotional Life of Your Brain *(with Richard J. Davidson, 2012). She has won numerous awards for her ability to explain complex scientific ideas to general audiences.*

What's in a Word? *(2009)*

Language may shape our thoughts.

When the Viaduct de Millau opened in the south of France in 2004, this tallest bridge in the world won worldwide accolades. German newspapers described how it "floated above the clouds" with "elegance and lightness" and "breathtaking" beauty. In France, papers praised the "immense" "concrete giant." Was it mere coincidence that the Germans saw beauty where the French saw heft and power? Lera Boroditsky thinks not.

A psychologist at Stanford University, she has long been intrigued by an age-old question whose modern form dates to 1956, when linguist Benjamin Lee Whorf asked whether the language we speak shapes the way we think and see the world. If so, then language is not merely a means of expressing thought, but a constraint on it, too. Although philosophers, anthropologists, and others have weighed in, with most concluding that language does not shape thought in any significant way, the field has been notable for a distressing lack of empiricism—as in testable hypotheses and actual data.

That's where Boroditsky comes in. In a series of clever experiments guided by pointed questions, she is amassing evidence that, yes, language shapes thought. The effect is powerful enough, she says, that "the private mental lives of speakers of different languages may differ dramatically," not only when they are thinking in order to speak, "but in all manner of cognitive tasks," including basic sensory perception. "Even a small fluke of grammar"—the gender of nouns—"can have an effect on how people think about things in the world," she says.

As in that bridge. In German, the noun for bridge, *Brucke*, is feminine. In French, *pont* is masculine. German speakers saw prototypically female features; French speakers, masculine ones. Similarly, Germans describe keys (*Schlussel*) with words such as hard, heavy, jagged, and metal, while to Spaniards keys

5

(*llaves*) are golden, intricate, little, and lovely. Guess which language construes key as masculine and which as feminine? Grammatical gender also shapes how we construe abstractions. In 85 percent of artistic depictions of death and victory, for instance, the idea is represented by a man if the noun is masculine and a woman if it is feminine, says Boroditsky. Germans tend to paint death as male, and Russians tend to paint it as female.

Language even shapes what we see. People have a better memory for colors if different shades have distinct names—not English's light blue and dark blue, for instance, but Russian's *goluboy* and *sinly*. Skeptics of the language-shapes-thought claim have argued that that's a trivial finding, showing only that people remember what they saw in both a visual form and a verbal one, but not proving that they actually see the hues differently. In an ingenious experiment, however, Boroditsky and colleagues showed volunteers three color swatches and asked them which of the bottom two was the same as the top one. Native Russian speakers were faster than English speakers when the colors had distinct names, suggesting that having a name for something allows you to perceive it more sharply. Similarly, Korean uses one word for "in" when one object is in another snugly (a letter in an envelope), and a different one when an object is in something loosely (an apple in a bowl). Sure enough, Korean adults are better than English speakers at distinguishing tight fit from loose fit.

In Australia, the Aboriginal Kuuk Thaayorre use compass directions for every spatial cue rather than right or left, leading to locutions such as "there is an ant on your southeast leg." The Kuuk Thaayorre are also much more skillful than English speakers at dead reckoning, even in unfamiliar surroundings or strange buildings. Their language "equips them to perform navigational feats once thought beyond human capabilities," Boroditsky wrote on Edge.org.

Science has only scratched the surface of how language affects thought. In Russian, verb forms indicate whether the action was completed or not—as in "she ate [and finished] the pizza." In Turkish, verbs indicate whether the action was observed or merely rumored. Boroditsky would love to run an experiment testing whether native Russian speakers are better than others at noticing if an action is completed, and if Turks have a heightened sensitivity to fact versus hearsay. Similarly, while English says "she broke the bowl" even if it smashed accidentally (she dropped something on it, say), Spanish and Japanese describe the same event more like "the bowl broke itself." "When we show people video of the same event," says Boroditsky, "English speakers remember who was to blame even in an accident, but Spanish and Japanese speakers remember it less well than they do intentional actions. It raises questions about whether language affects even something as basic as how we construct our ideas of causality."

Jonathan Kozol

Jonathan Kozol (1936–) has written a number of books on the issue of education. A graduate of Harvard University and a Rhodes Scholar at Oxford University, Kozol has taught at several schools, including Yale, and served as the Director of the National Literacy Coalition. His works include Death at an Early Age *(1967),* Rachel and Her Children *(1988),* Savage Inequalities *(1991), and* Amazing Grace: The Lives of Children and the Conscience of a Nation *(1996), among others.*

In the essay included here, from Kozol's 1985 volume Illiterate America, *the author explores how the issue of illiteracy impacts American society in a number of ways, one of which is a weakening of its democratic spirit.*

The Human Cost of an Illiterate Society (1985)

> *PRECAUTIONS, READ BEFORE USING.*
> *Poison: Contains sodium hydroxide (caustic soda-lye).*
> *Corrosive: Causes severe eye and skin damage, may cause blindness.*
> *Harmful or fatal if swallowed.*
> *If swallowed, give large quantities of milk or water.*
> *Do not induce vomiting.*
> *Important: Keep water out of can at all times to prevent contents*
> *from violently erupting. . . .*
>
> —Warning on a can of Drano

We are speaking here no longer of the dangers faced by passengers on Eastern Airlines or the dollar costs incurred by U.S. corporations and taxpayers. We are speaking now of human suffering and of the ethical dilemmas that are faced by a society that looks upon such suffering with qualified concern but does not take those actions which its wealth and ingenuity would seemingly demand.

Questions of literacy, in Socrates' belief, must at length be judged as matters of morality. Socrates could not have had in mind the moral compromise peculiar to a nation like our own. Some of our Founding Fathers did, however, have this question in their minds. One of the wisest of those Founding Fathers (one who may not have been most compassionate but surely was more prescient than some of his peers) recognized the special dangers that illiteracy would pose to basic equity in the political construction that he helped to shape.

"A people who mean to be their own governors," James Madison wrote, "must arm themselves with the power knowledge gives. A popular government without popular information or the means of acquiring it, is but a prologue to a farce or a tragedy, or perhaps both."

Tragedy looms larger than farce in the United States today. Illiterate citizens seldom vote. Those who do are forced to cast a vote of questionable worth. They cannot make informed decisions based on serious print information. Sometimes they can be alerted to their interests by aggressive voter education. More frequently, they vote for a face, a smile, or a style, not for a mind or character or body of beliefs.

5   The number of illiterate adults exceeds by 16 million the entire vote cast for the winner in the 1980 presidential contest. If even one third of all illiterates could vote, and read enough and do sufficient math to vote in their self-interest, Ronald Reagan would not likely have been chosen president. There is, of course, no way to know for sure. We do know this: Democracy is a mendacious term when used by those who are prepared to countenance the forced exclusion of one third of our electorate. So long as 60 million people are denied significant participation, the government is neither of, nor for, nor by, the people. It is a government, at best, of those two thirds whose wealth, skin color, or parental privilege allows them opportunity to profit from the provocation and instruction of the written word.

The undermining of democracy in the United States is one "expense" that sensitive Americans can easily deplore because it represents a contradiction that endangers citizens of all political positions. The human price is not so obvious at first.

Since I first immersed myself within this work I have often had the following dream: I find that I am in a railroad station or a large department store within a city that is utterly unknown to me and where I cannot understand the printed words. None of the signs or symbols is familiar. Everything looks strange: like mirror writing of some kind. Gradually I understand that I am in the Soviet Union. All the letters on the walls around me are Cyrillic. I look for my pocket dictionary but I find that it has been mislaid. Where have I left it? Then I recall that I forgot to bring it with me when I packed my bags in Boston. I struggle to remember the name of my hotel. I try to ask somebody for directions. One person stops and looks at me in a peculiar way. I lose the nerve to ask. At last I reach into my wallet for an ID card. The card is missing. Have I lost it? Then I remember that my card was confiscated for some reason, many years before. Around this point, I wake up in a panic.

This panic is not so different from the misery that millions of adult illiterates experience each day within the course of their routine existence in the U.S.A.

Illiterates cannot read the menu in a restaurant.

10   They cannot read the cost of items on the menu in the *window* of the restaurant before they enter.

Illiterates cannot read the letters that their children bring home from their teachers. They cannot study school department circulars that tell them of the courses that their children must be taking if they hope to pass the SAT exams. They cannot help with homework. They cannot write a letter to the teacher.

They are afraid to visit in the classroom. They do not want to humiliate their child or themselves.

Illiterates cannot read instructions on a bottle of prescription medicine. They cannot find out when a medicine is past the year of safe consumption; nor can they read of allergenic risks, warnings to diabetics, or the potential sedative effect of certain kinds of nonprescription pills. They cannot observe preventive health care admonitions. They cannot read about "the seven warning signs of cancer" or the indications of blood-sugar fluctuations or the risks of eating certain foods that aggravate the likelihood of cardiac arrest.

Illiterates live, in more than literal ways, an uninsured existence. They cannot understand the written details on a health insurance form. They cannot read the waivers that they sign preceding surgical procedures. Several women I have known in Boston have entered a slum hospital with the intention of obtaining a tubal ligation and have emerged a few days later after having been subjected to a hysterectomy. Unaware of their rights, incognizant of jargon, intimidated by the unfamiliar air of fear and atmosphere of ether that so many of us find oppressive in the confines even of the most attractive and expensive medical facilities, they have signed their names to documents they could not read and which nobody, in the hectic situation that prevails so often in those overcrowded hospitals that serve the urban poor, had even bothered to explain.

Childbirth might seem to be the last inalienable right of any female citizen within a civilized society. Illiterate mothers, as we shall see, already have been cheated of the power to protect their progeny against the likelihood of demolition in deficient public schools and, as a result, against the verbal servitude within which they themselves exist. Surgical denial of the right to bear that child in the first place represents an ultimate denial, an unspeakable metaphor, a final darkness that denies even the twilight gleamings of our own humanity. What greater violation of our biological, our biblical, our spiritual humanity could possibly exist than that which takes place nightly, perhaps hourly these days, within such overburdened and benighted institutions as the Boston City Hospital? Illiteracy has many costs; few are so irreversible as this.

Even the roof above one's head, the gas or other fuel for heating that protects the residents of northern city slums against the threat of illness in the winter months become uncertain guarantees. Illiterates cannot read the lease that they must sign to live in an apartment which, too often, they cannot afford. They cannot manage check accounts and therefore seldom pay for anything by mail. Hours and entire days of difficult travel (and the cost of bus or other public transit) must be added to the real cost of whatever they consume. Loss of interest on the check accounts they do not have, and could not manage if they did, must be regarded as another of the excess costs paid by the citizen who is excluded from the common instruments of commerce in a numerate society.

"I couldn't understand the bills," a woman in Washington, D.C., reports, "and then I couldn't write the checks to pay them. We signed things we didn't know what they were."

15

121

Illiterates cannot read the notices that they receive from welfare offices or from the IRS. They must depend on word-of-mouth instruction from the welfare worker—or from other persons whom they have good reason to mistrust. They do not know what rights they have, what deadlines and requirements they face, what options they might choose to exercise. They are half-citizens. Their rights exist in print but not in fact.

Illiterates cannot look up numbers in a telephone directory. Even if they can find the names of friends, few possess the sorting skills to make use of the yellow pages; categories are bewildering and trade names are beyond decoding capabilities for millions of nonreaders. Even the emergency numbers listed on the first page of the phone book—"Ambulance," "Police," and "Fire"—are too frequently beyond the recognition of nonreaders.

Many illiterates cannot read the admonition on a pack of cigarettes. Neither the Surgeon General's warning nor its reproduction on the package can alert them to the risks. Although most people learn by word of mouth that smoking is related to a number of grave physical disorders, they do not get the chance to read the detailed stories which can document this danger with the vividness that turns concern into determination to resist. They can see the handsome cowboy or the slim Virginia lady lighting up a filter cigarette; they cannot heed the words that tell them that this product is (not "may be") dangerous to their health. Sixty million men and women are condemned to be the unalerted, high-risk candidates for cancer.

20 Illiterates do not buy "no-name" products in the supermarkets. They must depend on photographs or the familiar logos that are printed on the packages of brand-name groceries. The poorest people, therefore, are denied the benefits of the least costly products.

Illiterates depend almost entirely upon label recognition. Many labels, however, are not easy to distinguish. Dozens of different kinds of Campbell's soup appear identical to the nonreader. The purchaser who cannot read and does not dare to ask for help, out of the fear of being stigmatized (a fear which is unfortunately realistic), frequently comes home with something which she never wanted and her family never tasted.

Illiterates cannot read instructions on a pack of frozen food. Packages sometimes provide an illustration to explain the cooking preparations; but illustrations are of little help to someone who must "boil water, drop the food—*within* its plastic wrapper—in the boiling water, wait for it to simmer, instantly remove."

Even when labels are seemingly clear, they may be easily mistaken. A woman in Detroit brought home a gallon of Crisco for her children's dinner. She thought that she had bought the chicken that was pictured on the label. She had enough Crisco now to last a year—but no more money to go back and buy the food for dinner.

Recipes provided on the packages of certain staples sometimes tempt a semi-literate person to prepare a meal her children have not tasted. The longing to vary the uniform and often starchy content of low-budget meals provided to the family that relies on food stamps commonly leads to ruinous results. Scarce funds have been wasted and the food must be thrown out. The same applies to distribution of food-surplus produce in emergency conditions. Government inducements to poor people to "explore the ways" by which to make a tasty meal from tasteless noodles, surplus cheese, and powdered milk are useless to nonreaders. Intended as benevolent advice, such recommendations mock reality and foster deeper feelings of resentment and of inability to cope. (Those, on the other hand, who cautiously refrain from "innovative" recipes in preparation of their children's meals must suffer the opprobrium of "laziness," "lack of imagination. . . .")

Illiterates cannot travel freely. When they attempt to do so, they encounter risks that few of us can dream of. They cannot read traffic signs and, while they often learn to recognize and to decipher symbols, they cannot manage street names which they haven't seen before. The same is true for bus and subway stops. While ingenuity can sometimes help a man or woman to discern directions from familiar landmarks, buildings, cemeteries, churches, and the like, most illiterates are virtually immobilized. They seldom wander past the streets and neighborhoods they know. Geographical paralysis becomes a bitter metaphor for their entire existence. They are immobilized in almost every sense we can imagine. They can't move up. They can't move out. They cannot see beyond. Illiterates may take an oral test for drivers' permits in most sections of America. It is a questionable concession. Where will they go? How will they get there? How will they get home? Could it be that some of us might like it better if they stayed where they belong?

Travel is only one of many instances of circumscribed existence. Choice, in almost all its facets, is diminished in the life of an illiterate adult. Even the printed TV schedule, which provides most people with the luxury of preselection, does not belong within the arsenal of options in illiterate existence. One consequence is that the viewer watches only what appears at moments when he happens to have time to turn the switch. Another consequence, a lot more common, is that the TV set remains in operation night and day. Whatever the program offered at the hour when he walks into the room will be the nutriment that he accepts and swallows. Thus, to passivity, is added frequency—indeed, almost uninterrupted continuity. Freedom to select is no more possible here than in the choice of home or surgery or food.

"You don't choose," said one illiterate woman. "You take your wishes from somebody else." Whether in perusal of a menu, selection of highways, purchase of groceries, or determination of affordable enjoyment, illiterate Americans must trust somebody else: a friend, a relative, a stranger on the street, a grocery clerk, a TV copywriter.

"All of our mail we get, it's hard for her to read. Settin' down and writing a letter, she can't do it. Like if we get a bill . . . we take it over to my sister-in-law. . . . My sister-in-law reads it."

Billing agencies harass poor people for the payment of the bills for purchases that might have taken place six months before. Utility companies offer an agreement for a staggered payment schedule on a bill past due. "You have to trust them," one man said. Precisely for this reason, you end up by trusting no one and suspecting everyone of possible deceit. A submerged sense of distrust becomes the corollary to a constant need to trust. "They are cheating me . . . I have been tricked . . . I do not know . . ."

30   *Not knowing:* This is a familiar theme. Not knowing the right word for the right thing at the right time is one form of subjugation. Not knowing the world that lies concealed behind those words is a more terrifying feeling. The longitude and latitude of one's existence are beyond all easy apprehension. Even the hard, cold stars within the firmament above one's head begin to mock the possibilities for self-location. Where am I? Where did I come from? Where will I go?

"I've lost a lot of jobs," one man explains. "Today, even if you're a janitor, there's still reading and writing . . . They leave a note saying, 'Go to room so-and-so . . .' You can't do it. You can't read it. You don't know."

"The hardest thing about it is that I've been places where I didn't know where I was. You don't know where you are . . . You're lost."

"Like I said: I have two kids. What do I do if one of my kids starts choking? I go running to the phone . . . I can't look up the hospital phone number. That's if we're at home. Out on the street, I can't read the sign. I get to a pay phone. 'Okay, tell us where you are. We'll send an ambulance.' I look at the street sign. Right there, I can't tell you what it says. I'd have to spell it out, letter for letter. By that time, one of my kids would be dead. . . . These are the kinds of fears you go with, every single day . . ."

"Reading directions, I suffer with. I work with chemicals. . . . That's scary to begin with . . ."

35   "You sit down. They throw the menu in front of you. Where do you go from there? Nine times out of ten you say, 'Go ahead. Pick out something for the both of us.' I've eaten some weird things, let me tell you!"

Menus. Chemicals. A child choking while his mother searches for a word she does not know to find assistance that will come too late. Another mother speaks about the inability to help her kids to read: "I can't read to them. Of course that's leaving them out of something they should have. Oh, it matters. You *believe* it matters! I ordered all these books. The kids belong to a book club. Donny wanted me to read a book to him. I told Donny: 'I can't read.' He said: 'Mommy, you sit down. I'll read it to you.' I tried it one day, reading from the pictures. Donny looked at me. He said, 'Mommy, that's not right.' He's only five. He knew I couldn't read . . .' "

A landlord tells a woman that her lease allows him to evict her if her baby cries and causes inconvenience to her neighbors. The consequence of challenging his words conveys a danger which appears, unlikely as it seems, even more alarming than the danger of eviction. Once she admits that she can't read, in the desire to maneuver for the time in which to call a friend, she will have defined herself in terms of an explicit impotence that she cannot endure. Capitulation in this case is preferable to self-humiliation. Resisting the definition of oneself in terms of what one cannot do, what others take for granted, represents a need so great that other imperatives (even one so urgent as the need to keep one's home in winter's cold) evaporate and fall away in face of fear. Even the loss of home and shelter, in this case, is not so terrifying as the loss of self.

"I come out of school. I was sixteen. They had their meetings. The directors meet. They said that I was wasting their school paper. I was wasting pencils . . ."

Another illiterate, looking back, believes she was not worthy of her teacher's time. She believes that it was wrong of her to take up space within her school. She believes that it was right to leave in order that somebody more deserving could receive her place.

Children choke. Their mother chokes another way: on more than chicken bones.   40

People eat what others order, know what others tell them, struggle not to see themselves as they believe the world perceives them. A man in California speaks about his own loss of identity, of self-location, definition:

"I stood at the bottom of the ramp. My car had broke down on the freeway. There was a phone. I asked for the police. They was nice. They said to tell them where I was. I looked up at the signs. There was one that I had seen before. I read it to them: ONE WAY STREET. They thought it was a joke. I told them I couldn't read. There was other signs above the ramp. They told me to try. I looked around for somebody to help. All the cars was going by real fast. I couldn't make them understand that I was lost. The cop was nice. He told me: 'Try once more.' I did my best. I couldn't read. I only knew the sign above my head. The cop was trying to be nice. He knew that I was trapped. 'I can't send out a car to you if you can't tell me where you are.' I felt afraid. I nearly cried. I'm forty-eight years old. I only said: 'I'm on a one-way street . . .'"

The legal problems and the courtroom complications that confront illiterate adults have been discussed above. The anguish that may underlie such matters was brought home to me this year while I was working on this book. I have spoken, in the introduction, of a sudden phone call from one of my former students, now in prison for a criminal offense. Stephen is not a boy today. He is twenty-eight years old. He called to ask me to assist him in his trial, which comes up next fall. He will be on trial for murder. He has just knifed and killed a man who first enticed him to his home, then cheated him, and then insulted him—as "an illiterate subhuman."

Stephen now faces twenty years to life. Stephen's mother was illiterate. His grandparents were illiterate as well. What parental curse did not destroy was killed off finally by the schools. Silent violence is repaid with interest. It will cost us $25,000 yearly to maintain this broken soul in prison. But what is the price that has been paid by Stephen's victim? What is the price that will be paid by Stephen?

Perhaps we might slow down a moment here and look at the realities   45
described above. This is the nation that we live in. This is a society that most of us did not create but which our President and other leaders have been willing to sustain by virtue of malign neglect. Do we possess the character and courage to address a problem which so many nations, poorer than our own, have found it natural to correct?

The answers to these questions represent a reasonable test of our belief in the democracy to which we have been asked in public school to swear allegiance.

Examining the Millennial Generation: Responding with Investigative Reports

College students who will graduate in 2014 and were born in or around 1992 are members of the Millennial Generation, also known as Generation Y. This generation shares many of the characteristics, viewpoints, and experiences that appear on the Beloit College Mindset List (www.beloit.edu/mindset). Ten of the seventy-five items of the list for the class of 2014 are shown on page 160, and just a glance at those items will tell you if you are a Millennial. If you are a first-year student who was born earlier than 1992 (like the great and growing number of those entering college as older adults) or later (like a number of advanced young people), you may not feel as though you share this mindset with your classmates.

At the start of each fall semester since 1998, Beloit College has released the Mindset List for the incoming college class, noting touchstones that have shaped the lives of that class. Created by Beloit's Keefer Professor of the Humanities Tom McBride and former Public Affairs Director Ron Nief, the Mindset List reminds faculty members of their dated references and of the experiences and values of their incoming students. For college faculty, the assassinations of Mohandas Gandhi, John F. Kennedy, Malcolm X, Robert F. Kennedy, Dr. Martin Luther King, Jr., and John Lennon may have marked critical moments in their younger lives; for incoming college students, those assassinations are ancient history, comparable to the assassinations of Abraham Lincoln or Julius Caesar.

AP Photo/Mark Humphrey

The Beloit College Mindset List for the Class of 2014

Most students entering college for the first time this fall—the Class of 2014—were born in 1992. For these students, Benny Hill, Sam Kinison, Sam Walton, Bert Parks and Tony Perkins have always been dead.

1. Few in the class know how to write in cursive.
2. E-mail is just too slow, and they seldom if ever use snail mail.
3. "Go West, Young College Grad" has always implied "and don't stop until you get to Asia . . . and learn Chinese along the way."
4. Al Gore has always been animated.
5. Los Angelenos have always been trying to get along.
6. Buffy has always been meeting her obligations to hunt down Lothos and the other blood-suckers at Hemery High.
7. "Caramel macchiato" and "venti half-caf vanilla latte" have always been street corner lingo.
8. With increasing numbers of ramps, Braille signs, and handicapped parking spaces, the world has always been trying harder to accommodate people with disabilities.
9. Had it remained operational, the villainous computer HAL could be their college classmate this fall, but they have a better chance of running into Miley Cyrus's folks on Parents' Weekend.
10. Entering college this fall in a country where a quarter of young people under 18 have at least one immigrant parent, they aren't afraid of immigration . . . unless it involves "real" aliens from another planet.

According to the Mindset List, "e-mail is just too slow" for the Millennials. Little wonder, then, that for this generation, doing just one thing at a time can seem outdated. The numerous distractions in the working and learning environments of Millennials and others close to their age provided a rhetorical opportunity for Christine Rosen, who published an investigative report titled "The Myth of Multitasking" (see pages 181–184). **Investigative reports** like Rosen's are commonly used to present the results of research. In her report, Rosen takes the opportunity to explain to readers the common perceptions—and misperceptions—about multitasking. At a time when far too many people celebrate their ability to multitask (and when employers may expect them to do it), Rosen analyzes the consequences of this behavior.

IDENTIFYING AN OPPORTUNITY

Throughout this chapter, you'll work to identify an opportunity to investigate a specific characteristic of the Millennials or of another generation. As you know, pundits are called on to hypothesize about up-and-coming generations for the mass media. As an investigative researcher, you will be doing more than hypothesizing: you will be making observations, conducting interviews, developing surveys, drawing from your personal experience, or doing library, online, or archival research and then presenting your findings to your audience. Whether or not you consider yourself a member of the Millennials, you can offer important insights or observations about a cultural touchstone, behavior, or value of a specific generation. As you work to determine what you want to investigate, consider the most fitting means of delivery for your report:

Print Report

written for a community or campus newspaper or local zine

Video Report

filmed for a campus television station or filmed and uploaded to YouTube

Online Report

for your online campus newspaper

To begin, freewrite for five minutes in response to each of the following questions (or use any of the invention techniques presented on pages 58–61):

1. Which physical spaces on your campus (or in your town) attract the Millennials—coffee shops, gyms, computer labs, multimedia labs, libraries? Do any of those spaces attract people of other generations as well? What physical spaces attract mostly students who are older or younger than the Millennials—study rooms, eating facilities, game rooms, sports areas? Describe a specific physical space and its inhabitants in as much detail as possible.

2. Consider the expectations of the Millennials (or students from an older or younger generation) on your campus. What particular services have been customized to meet those expectations? Think about career services, services for international students, academic services, and student life services as well as the offerings of the dining services and libraries. What specific evidence can you supply for your observation? Who might be interested in or disagree with your observation?

3. What would you like to know about the effects of the presence on your campus or in your community of the Millennial generation (or another older or younger generation)? Where might you begin researching for information to answer your question? Who, besides you, might be interested in what you find out?

4. What groups, both on campus and off, might be interested in or have a stake in the findings of an investigative report on the relationship between a specific generation and your school or your town? Make a list of the potential findings of an investigative report about Millennials (or another specific generation), based on what you've observed and experienced so far.

Real Situations

Though it may seem odd to label any generation, especially your own, consider the generational labels that have become common. The United States population contains a number of named generations: the Lost Generation, people who fought in or lived through World War I; the Greatest Generation, those who fought in World War II; the Silent Generation, those born between 1928 and 1945; the Baby Boomers, who were born after World War II, between 1946 and 1964; and Generation X, people born from 1965 through 1980. The very numerous

---

What's in a Name?

Generational names are the handiwork of popular culture. Some are drawn from a historic event; others from rapid social or demographic change; others from a big turn in the calendar.

The Millennial Generation falls into the third category. The label refers those born after 1980 – the first generation to come of age in the new millennium.

Generation X covers people born from 1965 through 1980. The label long ago overtook the first name affixed to this generation: the Baby Bust. Xers are often depicted as savvy, entrepreneurial loners.

The Baby Boomer label is drawn from the great spike in fertility that began in 1946, right after the end of World War II, and ended almost as abruptly in 1964, around the time the birth control pill went on the market. It's a classic example of a demography-driven name.

The Silent Generation describes adults born from 1928 through 1945. Children of the Great Depression and World War II, their "Silent" label refers to their conformist and civic instincts. It also makes for a nice contrast with the noisy ways of the anti-establishment Boomers.

The Greatest Generation (those born before 1928) "saved the world" when it was young, in the memorable phrase of Ronald Reagan. It's the generation that fought and won World War II.

Generational names are works in progress. The zeitgeist changes, and labels that once seemed spot-on fall out of fashion. It's not clear if the Millennial tag will endure, although a calendar change that comes along only once in a thousand years seems like a pretty secure anchor.

In 2010, the Pew Research Center published a report on the Millennials that included this list of generational names.

Pew Research Center's Social & Demographic Trends Project

Boomers created a cultural and economic phenomenon with their purchasing power and their rejection of traditional values. The Gen Xers have been considered to be without a clear identity, as their defining experiences have been instability (including the series of economic calamities since their birth and the high rate of divorce among their parents). Gen Xers were the first generation to take personal electronic devices for granted; home computers, cell phones, video games, and the Internet all became commonplace during their youth. The Millennial Generation, or Generation Y, characterized by the Beloit College Mindset List at the beginning of this chapter, consists of those born between about 1981 and the turn of the century. Following the Millennial Generation is Generation Z, or the Internet Generation, those who have never known a world without online capabilities.

The effects of such labels can spark strong reactions—for example, frustration in the Baby Boomers, whose name reminds people of the burden their large number will be for the Social Security system, and pride in the Greatest Generation, many of whom feel they deserve their tag, given their sacrifices during a world war and an economic depression. If you're a member of the Millennial Generation, you might resist the labels that pundits have applied to you and your cohort. You've been called "digital natives," which rings true only if the digital world is the only place you feel at home. Those among the Millennials who are the most digitally connected have been called "socially inept," because their obsession with online communication and entertainment often seems to have diminished their person-to-person, real-life social skills. If you're bristling at these labels, you might envy the positive attributes ascribed to members of earlier generations, especially since the Millennials have also been described as narcissistic and characterized as neither hard-working nor selfless. In contrast, the Millennials are also considered to be civic-minded (think about all the recent college graduates who have joined Teach for America) and better connected socially (with peers and older folks alike) than any other generation.

DESCRIBING THE MILLENNIAL GENERATION

1. How would you define the generation born between 1981 and 2001? Make a list of the distinguishing characteristics and cultural touchstones that you think define this generation.

2. How have you heard others define the generation born between 1981 and 2001? Work with a classmate or two to make a list of all the things you've heard about this generation. Be prepared to share your list with the rest of the class.

3. In what ways do the definitions from questions 1 and 2 overlap? Where do they diverge?

4. What do the images in this chapter suggest to you about the Millennials? What kind of visual is missing?

Real Responses to Real Situations

A number of writers have employed their available means to respond to rhetorical opportunities concerning the Millennial Generation. As you explore the responses presented here, ask yourself how what these writers have to say relates to your understanding of this generation. For example, if your parents are Baby Boomers, they know the feeling of having music, clothing, television, movies, education, and social policies fashioned to reflect and cater to their interests, estimated longevity, and spending capacity. Despite the raised eyebrows of their elders, their spending power, social freedoms, and seemingly unlimited educational and professional opportunities have allowed the Boomers to move optimistically forward with their lives. The same might be said of the Millennials.

Ted Horowitz

Millennials tend to get along well with their parents and others in older generations.

Defining a generation

Labeling generations has long been the norm, not surprisingly, since members of the same generation represent a demographic that can be both analyzed and exploited. Some generations have been named only after they have aged; the Greatest Generation is a case in point. But the Millennials were named early on and have been described in sometimes conflicting terms ever since. Even the span of their birth years (between 1981 and 2001, give or take a couple of years on either end) has been debated. In "The Millennial Muddle," award-winning writer Eric Hoover tells us that "figuring out young people has always been a chore, [and] today it's also an industry." He goes on to say that "colleges and corporations pay experts big bucks to help them understand the fresh-faced hordes that pack the nation's dorms and office buildings" and that "everyone in higher education has pondered 'The Millennials.'" Given the widespread and seemingly nonstop discussion of this generation, it is no surprise that a variety of opinions about it are in circulation. According to Hoover, depending on the so-called expert, "this generation either will save the planet, one soup kitchen at a time, or crash-land on a lonely moon where nobody ever reads." The Pew Research Center's report on the Millennials, whose overview is excerpted here, represents one of the positive depictions of this generation.

Excerpt from

> The Millennials: Confident. Connected. Open to Change.

Pew Research Center

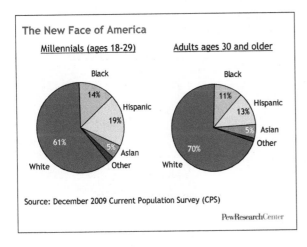

The New Face of America

Millennials (ages 18-29)

Adults ages 30 and older

Source: December 2009 Current Population Survey (CPS)

PewResearchCenter

Generations, like people, have personalities, and Millennials—the American teens and twenty-somethings who are making the passage into adulthood at the start of a new millennium—have begun to forge theirs: confident, self-expressive, liberal, upbeat and open to change.

They are more ethnically and racially diverse than older adults. They're less religious, less likely to have served in the military, and are on track to become the most educated generation in American history.

Their entry into careers and first jobs has been badly set back by the Great Recession, but they are more upbeat than their elders about their own economic futures as well as about the overall state of the nation.

They are history's first "always connected" generation. Steeped in digital technology and social media, they treat their multi-tasking hand-held gadgets almost like a body part—for better and worse. More than eight-in-ten say they sleep with a cell phone glowing by the bed, poised to disgorge texts, phone calls, e-mails, songs, news, videos, games and wake-up jingles. But sometimes convenience yields to temptation. Nearly two-thirds admit to texting while driving.

They embrace multiple modes of self-expression. Three-quarters have created a profile on a social networking site. One-in-five have posted a video of themselves online. Nearly four-in-ten have a tattoo (and for most who do, one is not enough: about half of those with tattoos have two to five and 18% have six or more). Nearly one-in-four have a piercing in some place other than an earlobe—about six times the share of older adults who've done this. But their look-at-me tendencies are not without limits. Most Millennials have placed privacy boundaries on their social media profiles. And 70% say their tattoos are hidden beneath clothing.

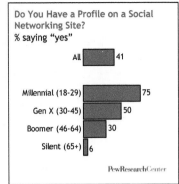

Do You Have a Profile on a Social Networking Site?
% saying "yes"

All 41
Millennial (18-29) 75
Gen X (30-45) 50
Boomer (46-64) 30
Silent (65+) 6

PewResearchCenter

Despite struggling (and often failing) to find jobs in the teeth of a recession, about nine-in-ten either say that they currently have enough money or that they will eventually meet their long-term financial goals. But [in early 2010], fully 37% of 18-to-29-year-olds are unemployed or out of the workforce, the highest share among this age group in more than three decades.

Whether as a by-product of protective parents, the age of terrorism or a media culture that focuses on dangers, they cast a wary eye on human nature. Two-thirds say "you can't be too careful" when dealing with people. Yet they are less skeptical than their elders of government. More so than other generations, they believe government should do more to solve problems.

They are the least overtly religious American generation in modern times. One-in-four are unaffiliated with any religion, far more than the share of older adults when they were ages 18 to 29. Yet not belonging does not necessarily mean not believing. Millennials pray about as often as their elders did in their own youth.

Only about six-in-ten were raised by both parents—a smaller share than was the case with older generations. In weighing their own life priorities, Millennials (like older adults) place parenthood and marriage far above career and financial success. But they aren't rushing to the altar. Just one-in-five Millennials (21%) are married now, half the share of their parents' generation at the same stage of life. About a third (34%) are parents.

Millennials are on course to become the most educated generation in American history, a trend driven largely by the demands of a modern knowledge-based economy, but most likely accelerated in recent years by the millions of 20-somethings enrolling in graduate schools, colleges or community colleges in part because they can't find a job. Among 18 to 24 year olds a record share—39.6%—was enrolled in college as of 2008, according to census data.

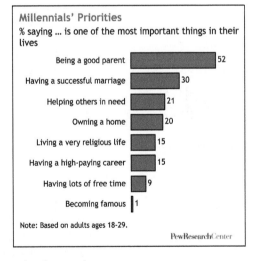

Millennials' Priorities
% saying … is one of the most important things in their lives

Being a good parent 52
Having a successful marriage 30
Helping others in need 21
Owning a home 20
Living a very religious life 15
Having a high-paying career 15
Having lots of free time 9
Becoming famous 1

Note: Based on adults ages 18-29.

PewResearchCenter

They get along well with their parents. Looking back at their teenage years, Millennials report having had fewer spats with mom or dad than older adults say they had with their own parents when they were growing up. And now, hard times have kept a significant share of adult Millennials and their parents under the same roof. About one-in-ten older Millennials (ages 22 and older) say they've "boomeranged" back to a parent's home because of the recession.

They respect their elders. A majority say that the older generation is superior to the younger generation when it comes to moral values and work ethic. Also, more than six-in-ten say that families have a responsibility to have an elderly parent come live with them if that parent wants to. By contrast, fewer than four-in-ten adults ages 60 and older agree that this is a family responsibility.

continued

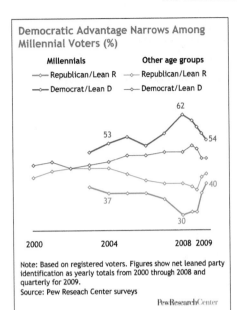

Democratic Advantage Narrows Among Millennial Voters (%)

Millennials · Republican/Lean R · Democrat/Lean D

Other age groups · Republican/Lean R · Democrat/Lean D

Note: Based on registered voters. Figures show net leaned party identification as yearly totals from 2000 through 2008 and quarterly for 2009.
Source: Pew Reseach Center surveys

PewResearchCenter

Despite coming of age at a time when the United States has been waging two wars, relatively few Millennials—just 2% of males—are military veterans. At a comparable stage of their life cycle, 6% of Gen Xer men, 13% of Baby Boomer men and 24% of Silent men were veterans.

Politically, Millennials were among Barack Obama's strongest supporters in 2008, backing him for president by more than a two-to-one ratio (66% to 32%) while older adults were giving just 50% of their votes to the Democratic nominee. This was the largest disparity between younger and older voters recorded in four decades of modern election day exit polling. Moreover, after decades of low voter participation by the young, the turnout gap in 2008 between voters under and over the age of 30 was the smallest it had been since 18- to 20-year-olds were given the right to vote in 1972.

But the political enthusiasms of Millennials have since cooled—for Obama and his message of change, for the Democratic Party and, quite possibly, for politics itself. About half of Millennials say the president has failed to change the way Washington works, which had been the central promise of his candidacy. Of those who say this, three-in-ten blame Obama himself, while more than half blame his political opponents and special interests.

To be sure, Millennials remain the most likely of any generation to self-identify as liberals; they are less supportive than their elders of an assertive national security policy and more supportive of a progressive domestic social agenda. They are still more likely than any other age group to identify as Democrats. Yet by early 2010, their support for Obama and the Democrats had receded, as evidenced both by survey data and by their low level of participation in recent off-year and special elections.

The Millennial Identity

Most Millennials (61%) in our January, 2010 survey say their generation has a unique and distinctive identity. That doesn't make them unusual, however. Roughly two-thirds of Silents, nearly six-in-ten Boomers and about half of Xers feel the same way about their generation.

But Millennials have a distinctive reason for feeling distinctive. In response to an open-ended follow-up question, 24% say it's because of their use of technology. Gen Xers also cite technology as their generation's biggest source of distinctiveness, but far fewer—just 12%—say this. Boomers' feelings of distinctiveness coalesce mainly around work ethic, which 17% cite as their most prominent identity badge. For Silents, it's the shared experience of the Depression and World War II, which 14% cite as the biggest reason their generation stands apart.

Millennials' technological exceptionalism is chronicled throughout the survey. It's not just their gadgets—it's the way they've fused their social lives into them. For example, three-quarters of Millennials have created a profile on a social networking site, compared with half of Xers, 30% of Boomers and 6% of Silents. There are big

---

What Makes Your Generation Unique?

	Millennial	Gen X	Boomer	Silent
1.	Technology use (24%)	Technology use (12%)	Work ethic (17%)	WW II, Depression (14%)
2.	Music/Pop culture (11%)	Work ethic (11%)	Respectful (14%)	Smarter (13%)
3.	Liberal/tolerant (7%)	Conservative/Trad'l (7%)	Values/Morals (8%)	Honest (12%)
4.	Smarter (6%)	Smarter (6%)	"Baby Boomers" (6%)	Work ethic (10%)
5.	Clothes (5%)	Respectful (5%)	Smarter (5%)	Values/Morals (10%)

Note: Based on respondents who said their generation was unique/distinct. Items represent individual, open-ended responses. Top five responses are shown for each age group. Sample sizes for sub-groups are as follows: Millennials, n=527; Gen X, n=173; Boomers, n=283; Silent, n=205.

---

generation gaps, as well, in using wireless technology, playing video games and posting self-created videos online. Millennials are also more likely than older adults to say technology makes life easier and brings family and friends closer together (though the generation gaps on these questions are relatively narrow).

Work Ethic, Moral Values, Race Relations

Of the four generations, Millennials are the only one that doesn't cite "work ethic" as one of their principal claims to distinctiveness. A nationwide Pew Research Center survey taken in 2009 may help explain why. This one focused on differences between young and old rather than between specific age groups. Nonetheless, its findings are instructive.

Nearly six-in-ten respondents cited work ethic as one of the big sources of differences between young and old. Asked who has the better work ethic, about three-fourths of respondents said that older people do. By similar margins, survey respondents also found older adults have the upper hand when it comes to moral values and their respect for others.

Do You Sleep with Your Cell Phone?
% who have ever placed their cell phone on or right next to their bed while sleeping

All	57
Millennial	83
Gen X	68
Boomer	50
Silent	20

PewResearchCenter

It might be tempting to dismiss these findings as a typical older adult gripe about "kids today." But when it comes to each of these traits—work ethic, moral values, respect for others—young adults *agree* that older adults have the better of it. In short, Millennials may be a self-confident generation, but they display little appetite for claims of moral superiority.

That 2009 survey also found that the public—young and old alike—thinks the younger generation is more racially tolerant than their elders. More than two decades of Pew Research surveys confirm that assessment. In their views about interracial dating, for example, Millennials are the most open to change of any generation, followed closely by Gen Xers, then Boomers, then Silents.

Likewise, Millennials are more receptive to immigrants than are their elders. Nearly six-in-ten (58%) say immigrants strengthen the country, according to a 2009 Pew Research survey; just 43% of adults ages 30 and older agree.

The same pattern holds on a range of attitudes about nontraditional family arrangements, from mothers of young children working outside the home, to adults living together without being married, to more people of different races marrying each other. Millennials are more accepting than older generations of these more modern family arrangements, followed closely by Gen Xers. To be sure, acceptance does not in all cases translate into outright approval. But it does mean Millennials disapprove less.

continued

The Millennials: Confident. Connected. Open to Change. *(continued)*

Weighing Trends in Marriage and Parenthood, by Generation
% saying this is a bad thing for society

	Millennial	Gen X	Boomer	Silent
More single women deciding to have children	59	54	65	72
More gay couples raising children	32	36	48	55
More mothers of young children working outside the home	23	29	39	38
More people living together w/o getting married	22	31	44	58
More people of different races marrying each other	5	10	14	26

Note: "Good thing", "Doesn't make much difference", and "Don't know" responses not shown.

A Gentler Generation Gap

A 1969 survey, taken near the height of the social and political upheavals of that turbulent decade, found that 74% of the public believed there was a "generation gap" in American society. Surprisingly, when that same question was asked in a Pew Research Center survey [in 2009]—in an era marked by hard economic times but little if any overt age-based social tension—the share of the public saying there was a generation gap had risen slightly to 79%.

But as the 2009 results also make clear, this modern generation gap is a much more benign affair than the one that cast a shadow over the 1960s. The public says this one is mostly about the different ways that old and young use technology—and relatively few people see that gap as a source of conflict. Indeed, only about a quarter of the respondents in the 2009 survey said they see big conflicts between young and old in America. Many more see conflicts between immigrants and the native born, between rich and poor, and between blacks and whites.

There is one generation gap that *has* widened notably in recent years. It has to do with satisfaction over the state of the nation. In recent decades the young have always tended to be a bit more upbeat than their elders on this key measure, but the gap is wider now than it has been in at least twenty years. Some 41% of Millennials say they are satisfied with the way things are going in the country, compared with just 26% of those ages 30 and older. Whatever toll a recession, a housing crisis, a financial meltdown and a pair of wars may have taken on the national psyche in the past few years, it appears to have hit the old harder than the young.

But this speaks to a difference in outlook and attitude; it's not a source of conflict or tension. As they make their way into adulthood, Millennials have already distinguished themselves as a generation that gets along well with others, especially their elders. For a nation whose population is rapidly going gray, that could prove to be a most welcome character trait.

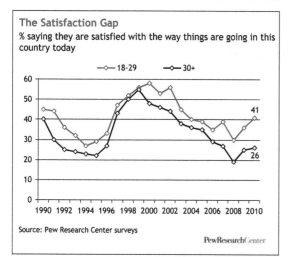

The Satisfaction Gap
% saying they are satisfied with the way things are going in this country today

Source: Pew Research Center surveys

PewResearchCenter

Author Derek Thompson, himself a member of the Millennial Generation, has written at length in an effort to define his generation, focusing on its members' personalities, outlooks, identities, maturation, employment problems and possibilities, education, and social practices and values. Thompson begins by summarizing the article to which he is responding, which provided his rhetorical opportunity.

> What's Really the Matter with 20-Somethings

© 2010. Reprinted by permission.
Derek Thompson

What is the deal with 20-somethings, these days? That's the question burning up the Internet and family room tables across the country since Robin Marantz Henig posed it in a mammoth *New York Times* **Magazine** article. In the last 30 years, Generation Y (or the Millennials) have pushed back each of the five milestones of adulthood: completing school, leaving home, becoming financially independent, marrying and having a child. We're not children, not yet adults, but rather in some Britney Spearsesque middle world of psychological development.

There are three levels to what author Henig calls "emerging adulthood." The first level is science and psychology: it's the idea that 20-somethings' brains and bodies might not be as grown up as we thought. The second level is today's culture: it's why Millennials, as opposed to all of history's young adults, are more likely to take time to "grow up." The third and final level is economic. The unemployment rate is 15.7 percent for workers aged 20 to 24. For 20-something African Americans and Hispanics without college degrees, that number is in the mid-20s. You can't become financially independent on food stamps.

The article mentions the bad economy only twice, both times by dismissing its impact ("it's a development that predates the current economic doldrums") to focus on developmental psychology. It's fine for the author Robin Marantz Henig to be more interested in science than economics.* But it's not fine for the *Times* Magazine to publish a front-page story called "What Is It About 20-Somethings?" when "it" is still the economy, stupid.

First, where Henig is correct: the bad economy has *accentuated* certain trends in the workforce rather than created a new generational identity overnight. Some of us were already delaying marrying and moving back with our parents before the recession. But some of these trends have nothing to do with our brains and everything to do with how we've chosen to use them.

Women and College
In 1970, women accounted for 36 percent of college graduates. Today they account for the majority. College educated women marry later, have fewer children, and are less likely to view marriage as "financial security," according to a

continued

---

*By the same token, since I am more interested and versed in economic trends than developmental psychology, this analysis might make too much of the recession and too little of brain development.

2010 Wharton study . . . . You can't explain delayed marriages and older mothers without talking about college.

Student Debt

Student debt recently eclipsed total credit card [debt] in this country at $860 billion. Before the recession, in 2006, the average public college student owed $17,250 from loans, according to the American Association of State Colleges and Universities. That number incredibly *doubled* from $8,000 in 1996. So put yourself in the shoes of a 22-year old from a relatively affluent family. You've graduated with $15,000 in debt, you can't find a job that pays more than $23,000 without benefits, and you don't hate your parents. Why *wouldn't* you live at home for a year?

Recession

Unemployment is 50 percent higher for 20-somethings than the general population. As *National Journal*'s Ron Brownstein has said, a functioning economy works like an escalator. You step on at high school, ascend through college, and step off into a decent paying job. But today, the escalator is jammed at the top. Senior workers won't leave their jobs because the recession devastated their 401(k) plans. Middle workers can't get promotions. And graduating seniors get stuck. Large employers hired 42 percent fewer graduating students in 2009, according to a Michigan State University study.

Something deeper is happening: it's the rise of a shadow job market without benefits or proper accounting. It's the emerging Freelancer Economy. Between 1995 and 2005, the number of self-employed independent contractors grew by 27 percent to almost 9 million workers. This phenomenon is especially prevalent in New York City, where self-employment accounted for two thirds of the job growth between 1975 and 2007, according to the Chicago Fed. Part-time jobs might be good for productivity and company output. But they come without health care or wage protection or the guarantee that they'll exist in a month. If we're moving slower toward adulthood, the economy is providing one hell of a headwind.

Half a century ago, it might have been normal to graduate from college (or not), marry in your lower 20s, have a kid, settle down at a nice firm, put in your 40 years and clock out with a good-looking pension. But that's not the world we live in. Horizontal mobility, part-time projects, rapidly changing jobs: this is the new normal. Maybe it's because we've been hopelessly coddled and our brains, with their flaccid synapses, have been massaged into thinking we could land our dream job at 23. Or! Maybe it's because the world changed, and it doesn't make sense to start a family at 24 in the shadow of $15,000 in debt with a thimbleful of jobs that don't provide health care or the promise of stability.

Henig's lengthy piece is impressive in its scope of developmental psychology and in its sensitivity to the question of whether 20-somethings need more help than we thought. Her concern is noted, and appreciated. But there are cultural and economic reasons why 20-somethings aren't growing up that have nothing to do with the pruning of our synapses. When people ask what's the matter with my generation, part of me wants to say: Have you seen the economy you created? *What's the matter with yours?*

But that's churlish. So instead, let's make a deal. Boomers, fix what you did to the country. And I promise you, the kids will be alright.

Currently director of the University Center for Innovation in Teaching and Education at Case Western Reserve University, theoretical physicist and social commentator Mano Singham regularly contributes to the *Chronicle of Higher Education*, where the following article originally appeared. A prolific writer (whose works include *God vs. Darwin: The War Between Evolution and Creationism in the Classroom*, *The Achievement Gap in US Education: Canaries in the Mine*, and *Quest for Truth: Scientific Progress and Religious Beliefs*), Singham posts his thoughts on subjects ranging from science, religion, and politics to the media, education, books, and film on his blog (http://blog.case.edu/singham).

> More than Millennials: Teachers Must Look Beyond Generational Stereotypes

Mano Singham

Until the 1990s, generations were thought by most people to span about 20 years, and labeling a generation with a catchy name usually meant that the cohort represented some major demographic trend. The births of the baby boomers, for example, had serious implications for social policy because of the need to project future needs in education, social services, and retirement. Giving that cohort an easily identifiable label made sense.

Now, however, it seems that a new generation is named every decade or less, driven by sweeping generalizations from the mass media and supported by little more than alleged changes in character traits as described by pop sociologists. One could dismiss all the generational splitting as the harmless fun of people in the news business, who need filler for their arts-and-style and pop-culture sections—except for the fact that it has seeped into academic conversations and may actually be influencing how we interact with college students, and not in a good way.

The first of the new breed of compressed generations was the so-called Generation X, consisting of those born after 1965, who are supposedly characterized by qualities of independence, resilience, and adaptability.

Tragically, before that generation could even reach its teenage years, it was killed off and replaced by Generation Y, consisting of those born after 1977. But it seems that Generation Y was unhappy with the label, and one can understand why. The letter X carries with it an aura of mystery, while Y is merely the letter after X, always playing second fiddle. Even in graphs, X is the independent variable, adventurously staking out new ground, while Y is the plodding dependent variable, following along in X's wake. Who wants to be part of that crowd? So Generation Y was rechristened as the Millennials, a catchy title for those coming of age at the turn of the century, and it has stuck.

And what do we know about these Millennials? A lot, it seems. Here's one description, from "Generation X and the Millennials: What You Need to Know

continued

About Mentoring the New Generations," by Diane Thielfoldt and Devon Scheef:

> The 75 million members of this generation are being raised at the most child-centric time in our history. Perhaps it's because of the showers of attention and high expectations from parents that they display a great deal of self-confidence. . . . Millennials are typically team-oriented, banding together to date and socialize. . . . They work well in groups, preferring this to individual endeavors. They're good multitaskers, having juggled sports, school, and social interests as children, so expect them to work hard. Millennials seem to expect structure in the workplace. They acknowledge and respect positions and titles, and want a relationship with their boss. . . . They are definitely in need of mentoring. . . . and they'll respond well to the personal attention. Because they appreciate structure and stability, mentoring Millennials should be more formal, with set meetings and a more authoritative attitude on the mentor's part.

Really? We seem to have those 75 million people pegged, don't we?

The Millennial label was so successful that we were loath to let it go, so that generation was allowed to grow into adulthood until 1998, when the news media decided that it was time for a new one. Generation Z was thus born, comprising those born from the mid- to late-1990s through the 2000s. Their arrival is now indelibly linked with the events of September 11, 2001, and Generation Z's worldview is supposedly shaped by that one event.

But that's not all. With the source of generation labels shifting from demographics to character traits and the influence of significant contemporaneous events, we have now gone back in time and cut earlier generations into more finely grained slices that encompass smaller age cohorts. Generation Next consists of people born between 1982 and 1989 who, according to the Pew Research Center, "have grown up with personal computers, cell phones, and the Internet and are now taking their place in a world where the only constant is rapid change." The MTV Generation consists of those who occupy the space between Generation X and Generation Y. Even the venerable baby boomers have succumbed to this generational Balkanization, with those born between 1954 and 1965 being peeled off and given their own enigmatic label of Generation Jones. Why? Because late boomers are presumed to have been too young to be deeply affected by the Vietnam War and Woodstock—supposedly the cultural touchstones that shaped the worldview of early boomers.

I suspect that student-life and admissions administrators are the first to be influenced by such generational bandwagons. They have to deal with parents and with students' nonacademic lives, and thus must keep their antennae tuned to what is going [on] in popular culture. From them these terms diffuse into general university conversation.

I attended a conference on college teaching recently and was amazed at how often generational stereotypes were brought up and used as a valid basis for dealing with students. All it took was one person dropping the word "Millennial" into the discussion, and the anecdotes started pouring out: The students who demand instant gratification, those who send repeated e-mail messages to their professors in the middle of the night and are annoyed when they don't get an immediate reply, those who expect professors to give them a wake-up call on field trips because that is what their parents did, those whose parents cling to them and intercede on their behalf, those who cling to their parents, those who confide intimate details about their lives that professors need not (and would rather not) know, those who demand to be told exactly what they need to do on assignments, and so on. Such stories seem to spring from an inexhaustible well. And the picture of the Millennials that emerges is that of a whiny, needy, instant-gratification-seeking, grade-oriented bunch of students.

It should be borne in mind that those stories were not told by bitter, curmudgeonly, "you kids get off my lawn!"-type professors who hate being in the company of students and think that universities would be much better places if no pesky undergraduates were around to interrupt the day. The puzzle is that the people who attend such teaching conferences and make such comments are often some of the best and most caring teachers—the ones who are constantly trying to find ways to improve their teaching and reach more students.

The willingness of such professors to accept generational stereotypes stands in stark contrast to their sensitivity when it comes to gender and ethnic stereotypes. During one session on identifying and dealing with classroom incivilities, a couple of professors ventured the suggestion that what students considered incivil may depend on their culture: that Korean students may unwittingly commit plagiarism because they believe that citing sources is an insult to their professor; that Saudi Arabian students like to negotiate grades with their professors because they come from a bargaining culture; that Latin American students think that something is cheating only if you get caught. There was immediate pushback from other professors that such generalizations are not valid—and are in fact harmful, because they prevent us from seeing the individuality in students. Generalizations about the Millennials, however, went unchallenged.

Why are we in academe so accepting of media-driven constructs like the ever-multiplying generation labels? Paradoxically, it may be because we want to help students. Thoughtful academics are problem solvers, and when dealing with disengaged students, giving the problem a label gives one the sense that one understands it and can set about dealing with it.

But generational stereotypes are of no value for professors—and not because they are entirely false. After all, stereotypes are usually based on some reality. But even if different populations exhibit, on average, their own distinct traits, large populations like nations and generations include so many deviations from the norm that stereotypes are of little use in predicting the traits that any given person is likely to display.

It would be silly to argue that student behavior hasn't changed over time. But what we are observing may not be a result of new traits emerging, but rather old traits manifesting themselves in novel forms because of changes in external conditions. Maybe parents have not become more clingy or students more psychologically dependent on them. Perhaps the truth is simply that college has become vastly more complicated and difficult to navigate, with its explosion of majors, minors, and other programs—not to mention the byzantine rules for financial aid—so perhaps some parents have felt obliged to step in more than they might have in earlier generations to act on their children's behalf.

Similarly, we have always had students who were uninhibited, socially awkward, or needed instant gratification. But now e-mail and Facebook enable them to

continued

More than Millennials: Teachers Must Look Beyond Generational Stereotypes *(continued)*

display those qualities in ways they couldn't before—such as by expecting immediate responses to midnight queries or revealing personal information online they should keep to themselves.

Students are diverse and have always been diverse. I've taught for over three decades and have my own cache of funny or poignant stories about needy, annoying, or self-absorbed students. We teachers love stories about students, and treasure and accumulate them like anglers or golfers do about their pastimes. While my own stories can fit those spread around about the Millennials, many of them are about students from long ago, before it became fashionable to label students according to their birth years.

Bertrand Russell said that "no man can be a good teacher unless he has feelings of warm affection toward his pupils and a genuine desire to impart to them what he himself believes to be of value." The trouble with generational stereotyping is that it sucks the individuality out of our students, the very thing that generates those feelings of warm affection. It makes them into generic types, whose personalities and motivations we think we can discern without having to go to all the bother of actually getting to know them.

> ANALYZING THE RHETORICAL SITUATION

1. To what rhetorical opportunity is each of the three pieces of writing in this section responding?
2. What characteristic of the Millennial Generation does each piece of writing investigate?
3. Who is the specific audience for each of the three pieces? For what purpose was each written? How do the purpose and audience of each piece connect?
4. What facts and evidence does each piece of writing present to help readers better understand the Millennials? What kinds of research do you think were needed to find those facts and that evidence?
5. How do each of these pieces draw on the rhetorical appeals of ethos, logos, and pathos to support opinions about the Millennials? Work with another classmate or two to find passages from each of the texts to support your answers. Be prepared to share your answers with the rest of the class.

Investigating what it means to grow up in a digital world

Most college students are fluent digital communicators, whether they use hand-held devices, touch-screen devices, or personal computers. As one of those students, your expertise has likely been forged by long use of electronic devices, perhaps starting with a desktop computer. Although some experts argue that people who rely on electronic communication do so at the expense of their person-to-person social skills, you might not agree. In fact, your own life may prove that just the opposite is true. You might be one of those people who mails out personalized, handwritten holiday cards every winter. Between envelope-addressing sessions, you might check your e-mail and Facebook accounts to see who has accepted an invitation to the annual holiday party—at your home, at your place of worship, or at one of your social clubs, where you see and talk with your friends and associates face to face. Just because you're digitally savvy doesn't necessarily mean you're socially inept; the two qualities are not mutually exclusive.

The following articles explore the complicated cause-and-consequence relationships between the use of digital methods of communication and the users' social and educational lives. David Fallarme, the author of the first article, is a digital marketing professional, consultant to businesses, and author of the blog *The Marketing Student.*

> A Look at How Gen Y Communicates

Used by permission.
David Fallarme

Boomers had it pretty simple back in their youth. Want to connect with your friends? Write them a letter, give them a call or go and see them.

Postal mail   Phone call   Face to Face

URGENCY →

David Fallarme

Gen X-ers had a little more fun. They could've e-mailed each other over 28.8 [phone-line dial-up for the Internet] or used their pagers to send 1-sentence messages back and forth.

Postal mail   Email   Beeper   Phone call   Face to Face

URGENCY →

David Fallarme

continued

A Look at How Gen Y Communicates *(continued)*

Here's what **Generation Y** uses to stay in touch.

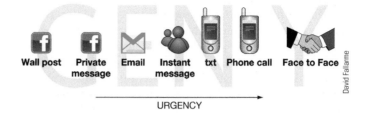

To an outsider, it can be confusing to understand how Gen Y uses those channels just to talk to each other. After all, Boomers just had three channels and they made friends just fine. To put things in context, here's what my communication habits are like and how I use the above.

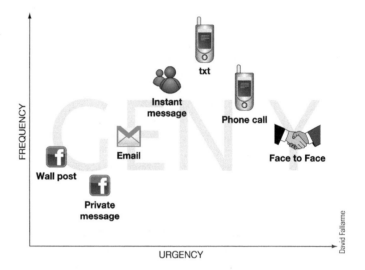

Looking at that chart makes me envy my father's generation. They didn't have to worry about drunk texts. Or having personal information all over the internet.

In the following essay, Mark Bauerlein, professor of English at Emory University, writes about the problems Millennials have in face-to-face social situations. A specialist in American culture, Professor Bauerlein has written widely on civil rights, race riots, and Walt Whitman. In addition, he regularly contributes to such publications as the *Wall Street Journal,* the *Washington Post,* and the *Chronicle of Higher Education.* His latest book is *The Dumbest Generation: How the Digital Age Stupefies Young Americans and Jeopardizes Our Future (Or, Don't Trust Anyone Under 30).*

> Why Gen-Y Johnny Can't Read Non-Verbal Cues

Mark Bauerlein

In September 2008, when Nielsen Mobile announced that teenagers with cellphones each sent and received, on average, 1,742 text messages a month, the number sounded high, but just a few months later Nielsen raised the tally to 2,272. A year earlier, the National School Boards Association estimated that middle- and high-school students devoted an average of nine hours to social networking each week. Add e-mail, blogging, IM, tweets and other digital customs and you realize what kind of hurried, 24/7 communications system young people experience today.

Affordable Illustration Source/Images.com/Getty Images

Unfortunately, nearly all of their communication tools involve the exchange of written words alone. At least phones, cellular and otherwise, allow the transmission of tone of voice, pauses and the like. But even these clues are absent in the text-dependent world. Users insert smiley-faces into e-mails, but they don't see each others' actual faces. They read comments on Facebook, but they don't "read" each others' posture, hand gestures, eye movements, shifts in personal space and other nonverbal—and expressive—behaviors.

Back in 1959, anthropologist Edward T. Hall labeled these expressive human attributes "the Silent Language." Hall passed away last month in Santa Fe at age 95, but his writings on nonverbal communication deserve continued attention. He argued that body language, facial expressions and stock mannerisms function "in juxtaposition to words," imparting feelings, attitudes, reactions and judgments in a different register.

This is why, Hall explained, U.S. diplomats could enter a foreign country fully competent in the native language and yet still flounder from one miscommunication to another, having failed to decode the manners, gestures and subtle protocols that go along with words. And how could they, for the "silent language" is acquired through acculturation, not schooling. Not only is it unspoken; it is largely unconscious. The meanings that pass through it remain implicit, more felt than understood.

They are, however, operative. Much of our social and workplace lives runs on them. For Hall, breakdowns in nonverbal communication took place most damagingly in cross-cultural circumstances—for instance, federal workers dealing with Navajo Indians and misconstruing their basic conceptions of time. Within cultures, Hall assumed, people more or less "spoke" the same silent language.

They may no longer, thanks to the avalanche of all-verbal communication. In Silicon Valley itself, as the Los Angeles Times reported last year, some companies have installed the "topless" meeting—in which not only laptops but iPhones and other tools are banned—to combat a new problem: "continuous partial attention." With a device close by, attendees at workplace meetings simply cannot keep their focus on the speaker. It's too easy to check e-mail, stock quotes and Facebook. While a quick log-on may seem, to the user, a harmless break, others in the room receive it as a silent dismissal. It announces: "I'm not interested." So the tools must now remain at the door.

continued

Older employees might well accept such a ban, but younger ones might not understand it. Reading a text message in the middle of a conversation isn't a lapse to them—it's what you do. It has, they assume, no nonverbal meaning to anyone else.

It does, of course, but how would they know it? We live in a culture where young people—outfitted with iPhone and laptop and devoting hours every evening from age 10 onward to messaging of one kind and another—are ever less likely to develop the "silent fluency" that comes from face-to-face interaction. It is a skill that we all must learn, in actual social settings, from people (often older) who are adept in the idiom. As text-centered messaging increases, such occasions diminish. The digital natives improve their adroitness at the keyboard, but when it comes to their capacity to "read" the behavior of others, they are all thumbs.

Nobody knows the extent of the problem. It is too early to assess the effect of digital habits, and the tools change so quickly that research can't keep up with them. By the time investigators design a study, secure funding, collect results and publish them, the technology has changed and the study is outdated.

Still, we might reasonably pose questions about silent-language acquisition in a digital environment. Lots of folks grumble about the diffidence, self-absorption and general uncommunicativeness of Generation Y. The next time they face a twenty-something who doesn't look them in the eye, who slouches and sighs for no apparent reason, who seems distracted and unaware of the rising frustration of the other people in the room, and who turns aside to answer a text message with glee and facility, they shouldn't think, "What a rude kid." Instead, they should show a little compassion and, perhaps, seize on a teachable moment. "Ah," they might think instead, "another texter who doesn't realize that he is communicating, right now, with every glance and movement—and that we're reading him all too well."

Prolific writer and artist Laurie Fendrich is professor at Hofstra University, where she teaches courses in drawing, painting, humanities, and art appreciation. Her own artwork (paintings, drawings, and installations) has appeared in galleries all over North America. Her productive professional life also includes writing, which she does regularly for the *Chronicle of Higher Education.* Her view of the Millennial Generation seems more respectful and sympathetic than the views of some of her contemporaries.

> Bad Student Writing? Not So Fast!

Reprinted by permission.

Laurie Fendrich

It would be good for the blood pressure of everyone involved in criticizing education—state legislators, education policy professionals, professors, school administrators, parents—to take a deep breath. Put aside the statistics, the studies, the anecdotes, and take a look at the big picture.

Here's what Edith Hamilton had to say about education, in *The Echo of Greece* (1957), one of her many trenchant books on the subject of the ancient Greeks:

> If people feel that things are going from bad to worse and look at the new generation to see if they can be trusted to take charge among such dangers, they invariably conclude that they cannot and that these irresponsible young people have not been trained properly. Then the cry goes up, "What is wrong with our education?" and many answers are always forthcoming.

Note the droll and ironic, "and many answers are always forthcoming." Perhaps studying people who lived so long ago—people who invented the very idea of education as a route to genuine freedom, and understood freedom to be worthwhile only when coupled with self-control—gave Hamilton one of those calm, stoical uber-minds that comprehends competing pronouncements about education never to be more than opinion.

While the rest of us thrash about interpreting the parade of studies and tests demonstrating that students can no longer think, read, write, do math, know the dates of the Civil War or the fall of Byzantium, or identify a water molecule when it's softly floating on a glass slide, Hamilton calmly sees 'twas ever thus. In an interesting aside, she also observes that there's an increase in "educational fervor" whenever there's a lack of confidence in the state.

I'd go further. The problem of "control freaks" applies to generations as well as to individuals. Older generations never voluntarily let go. They embrace new ideas only grudgingly, and often won't even try to understand the younger generation they themselves spawned. One of the many tragedies of existence is that the only species that's equipped by nature to have back-and-forth conversations between generations resists such conversations with all its might.

Clive Thompson's article on the "new literacy" (*Wired Magazine*, 24 August [2011]) urges those of us who are fretting about the decline in writing, in particular, to buck up. Unlike Hamilton, who points to the eternal past for comfort, Thompson points to the present and the future. He reports on a large, ongoing study at Stanford—the Stanford Study of Writing—directed by Andrea Lunsford, a professor of writing and rhetoric at Stanford University. Her conclusion? "I think we're in the midst of a literacy revolution the likes of which we haven't seen since Greek civilization."

Thompson writes, "Technology isn't killing our ability to write. It's reviving it—and pushing our literacy in bold new directions." The Stanford study, although incomplete, already shows that young people today write far, far more than any previous generation, and a lot of it they do outside the classroom (!).

While the older generation worries endlessly (frequently employing pretentious prose in the process) over the quality of the writing on Facebook, blogs and Twitter, the younger generation enthusiastically probes new ways to express themselves clearly and concisely (texting and Twitter), to exchange open opinions about every matter under the sun (Twitter and Facebook), and to do all these things in clever, inventive ways. Lunsford sees a link between the modern world of online writing—feisty, conversational, out in public, and concise—and the ancient Greek tradition of argument.

What if the younger generation ends up better writers than their parents—and their professors? Perish the thought!

> ANALYZING THE RHETORICAL SITUATION

1. To what rhetorical opportunity are David Fallarme, Mark Bauerlein, and Laurie Fendrich each responding?
2. What specific argument does each writer appear to be making?
3. Fendrich urges readers to "Put aside the statistics, the studies, the anecdotes, and take a look at the big picture." What point do you think she is making about those kinds of evidence? What kinds of details and evidence does she use to support her argument? Work with another classmate or two to compose your answers and be prepared to share them with the rest of the class.

COMMUNITY CONNECTIONS

1. Write for ten minutes in response to one of the pieces you've just read about the effects of the use of technology. How do the descriptions or examples offered by the writer coincide with or diverge from your own experiences?

2. Chart your use of communication technologies in the way that David Fallarme does (in terms of frequency and urgency). How often are you prompted to interpret nonverbal communication when using technology? How often do you rely solely on writing when using communication technology?

3. Write for ten minutes about the causes or the consequences of using one type of communication technology. Work with another classmate or two to determine which communication technology you'll focus on. Be prepared to share your list of causes or consequences with the rest of the class.

Investigative Reports: A Fitting Response

As many of the pieces of writing in this chapter demonstrate, an investigative report can sometimes be the most fitting response to a rhetorical opportunity. Each of the pieces is a response to the question of what characterizes the Millennial Generation. Because there is vigorous disagreement about the definition of that generation, each of the authors conducted research (library, experiential, observational, or online) to support his or her findings. Thus, their pieces *define* the nature of the Millennial Generation, *clarify* how this generation can be distinguished from other generations, and *illustrate* a conception of the Millennials with examples.

A report investigating the causes and consequences of multitasking

In her investigative report, which appeared in *The New Atlantis: A Journal of Technology & Society*, Christine Rosen explores what is really happening in our brains when we try to pay attention to many things at once. She uses cause-and-consequence analysis to organize her piece.

The Myth of Multitasking

Christine Rosen

In one of the many letters he wrote to his son in the 1740s, Lord Chesterfield offered the following advice: "There is time enough for everything in the course of the day, if you do but one thing at once, but there is not time enough in the year, if you will do two things at a time." To Chesterfield, singular focus was not merely a practical way to structure one's time; it was a mark of intelligence. "This steady and undissipated attention to one object, is a sure mark of a superior genius; as hurry, bustle, and agitation, are the never-failing symptoms of a weak and frivolous mind."

In modern times, hurry, bustle, and agitation have become a regular way of life for many people—so much so that we have embraced a word to describe our efforts to respond to the many pressing demands on our time: *multitasking*. Used for decades to describe the parallel processing abilities of computers, multitasking is now shorthand for the human attempt to do simultaneously as many things as possible, as quickly as possible, preferably marshalling the power of as many technologies as possible.

In the late 1990s and early 2000s, one sensed a kind of exuberance about the possibilities of multitasking. Advertisements for new electronic gadgets—particularly the first generation of handheld digital devices—celebrated the notion of using technology to accomplish several things at once. The word *multitasking* began appearing in the "skills" sections of résumés, as office workers restyled themselves as high-tech, high-performing team players. "We have always multitasked—inability to walk and chew gum is a time-honored cause for derision—but never so intensely or self-consciously as now," James Gleick wrote in his 1999 book *Faster*. "We are multitasking connoisseurs—experts in crowding, pressing, packing, and overlapping distinct activities in our all-too-finite moments." An article in the *New York Times Magazine* in 2001 asked, "Who can remember life before multitasking? These days we all do it." The article offered advice on "How to Multitask" with suggestions about giving your brain's "multitasking hot spot" an appropriate workout.

But more recently, challenges to the ethos of multitasking have begun to emerge. Numerous studies have shown the sometimes-fatal danger of using cell phones and other electronic devices while driving, for example, and several states have now made that particular form of multitasking illegal. In the business world, where concerns about time-management are perennial, warnings about workplace distractions spawned by a multitasking culture are on the rise. In 2005, the BBC reported on a research study, funded by Hewlett-Packard and conducted by the Institute of Psychiatry at the University of London, that found, "Workers distracted by e-mail and phone calls suffer a fall in IQ more than twice

Rosen begins with age-old advice about the wisdom of doing things one at a time. She has identified a rhetorical opportunity for addressing a modern-day problem.

Rosen defines her topic in precise terms: multitasking has become a way of life, or at least an expectation.

Rosen provides historical background on multitasking, including differing perspectives on this behavior. She starts with a positive perspective.

Rosen moves to a discussion of negative perspectives. She uses direct quotations to help convey those perspectives.

Evidence from careful research helps Rosen establish her ethos and enhances the logos of her overall argument.

that found in marijuana smokers." The psychologist who led the study called this new "infomania" a serious threat to workplace productivity. One of the *Harvard Business Review*'s "Breakthrough Ideas" for 2007 was Linda Stone's notion of "continuous partial attention," which might be understood as a subspecies of multitasking: using mobile computing power and the Internet, we are "constantly scanning for opportunities and staying on top of contacts, events, and activities in an effort to miss nothing."

Dr. Edward Hallowell, a Massachusetts-based psychiatrist who specializes in the treatment of attention deficit/hyperactivity disorder and has written a book with the self-explanatory title *CrazyBusy*, has been offering therapies to combat extreme multitasking for years; in his book he calls multitasking a "mythical activity in which people believe they can perform two or more tasks simultaneously." In a 2005 article, he described a new condition, "Attention Deficit Trait," which he claims is rampant in the business world. ADT is "purely a response to the hyperkinetic environment in which we live," writes Hallowell, and its hallmark symptoms mimic those of ADD. "Never in history has the human brain been asked to track so many data points," Hallowell argues, and this challenge "can be controlled only by creatively engineering one's environment and one's emotional and physical health." Limiting multitasking is essential. Best-selling business advice author Timothy Ferriss also extols the virtues of "single-tasking" in his book, *The 4-Hour Workweek*.

Multitasking might also be taking a toll on the economy. One study by researchers at the University of California at Irvine monitored interruptions among office workers; they found that workers took an average of twenty-five minutes to recover from interruptions such as phone calls or answering e-mail and return to their original task. Discussing multitasking with the *New York Times* in 2007, Jonathan B. Spira, an analyst at the business research firm Basex, estimated that extreme multitasking—information overload—costs the U.S. economy $650 billion a year in lost productivity.

Changing Our Brains

To better understand the multitasking phenomenon, neurologists and psychologists have studied the workings of the brain. In 1999, Jordan Grafman, chief of cognitive neuroscience at the National Institute of Neurological Disorders and Stroke (part of the National Institutes of Health), used functional magnetic resonance imaging (fMRI) scans to determine that when people engage in "task-switching"—that is, multitasking behavior—the flow of blood increases to a region of the frontal cortex called Brodmann area 10. (The flow of blood to particular regions of the brain is taken as a proxy indication of activity in those regions.) "This is presumably the last part of the brain to evolve, the most mysterious and exciting part," Grafman told the *New York Times* in 2001—adding, with a touch of hyperbole, "It's what makes us most human."

Citing a wide range of credited sources helps Rosen convey to readers that she has conducted a fair, balanced investigation.

It is also what makes multitasking a poor long-term strategy for learning. Other studies, such as those performed by psychologist René Marois of Vanderbilt University, have used fMRI to demonstrate the brain's response to handling multiple tasks. Marois found evidence of a "response selection bottleneck" that occurs when the brain is forced to respond to several stimuli at once. As a result, task-switching leads to time lost as the brain determines which task to perform. Psychologist David Meyer at the University of Michigan believes that rather than a bottleneck in the brain, a process of "adaptive executive control" takes place, which "schedules task processes appropriately to obey instructions about their relative priorities and serial order," as he described to the *New Scientist*. Unlike many other researchers who study multitasking, Meyer is optimistic that, with training, the brain can learn to task-switch more effectively, and there is some evidence that certain simple tasks are amenable to such practice. But his research has also found that multitasking contributes to the release of stress hormones and adrenaline, which can cause long-term health problems if not controlled, and contributes to the loss of short-term memory.

In one recent study, Russell Poldrack, a psychology professor at the University of California, Los Angeles, found that "multitasking adversely affects how you learn. Even if you learn while multitasking, that learning is less flexible and more specialized, so you cannot retrieve the information as easily." His research demonstrates that people use different areas of the brain for learning and storing new information when they are distracted: brain scans of people who are distracted or multitasking show activity in the striatum, a region of the brain involved in learning new skills; brain scans of people who are not distracted show activity in the hippocampus, a region involved in storing and recalling information. Discussing his research on National Public Radio recently, Poldrack warned, "We have to be aware that there is a cost to the way that our society is changing, that humans are not built to work this way. We're really built to focus. And when we sort of force ourselves to multitask, we're driving ourselves to perhaps be less efficient in the long run even though it sometimes feels like we're being more efficient."

If, as Poldrack concluded, "multitasking changes the way people learn," what might this mean for today's children and teens, raised with an excess of new entertainment and educational technology, and avidly multitasking at a young age? Poldrack calls this the "million-dollar question." Media multitasking—that is, the simultaneous use of several different media, such as television, the Internet, video games, text messages, telephones, and e-mail—is clearly on the rise, as a 2006 report from the Kaiser Family Foundation showed: in 1999, only 16 percent of the time people spent using any of those media was spent on multiple media at once; by 2005, 26 percent of media time was spent multitasking. "I multitask every single second I am online," confessed one study participant. "At this very moment I am watching TV, checking my e-mail every two minutes, reading a newsgroup about who shot JFK, burning some music to a CD, and writing this message."

The Kaiser report noted several factors that increase the likelihood of media multitasking, including "having a computer and being able to see a television from it." Also, "sensation-seeking" personality types are more likely to multitask, as are those living in "a highly TV-oriented household." The picture that emerges of these pubescent multitasking mavens is of a generation of great technical facility and intelligence but of extreme impatience, unsatisfied with slowness and uncomfortable with silence: "I get bored if it's not all going at once, because everything has gaps—waiting for a website to come up, commercials on TV, etc." one participant said. The report concludes on a very peculiar note, perhaps intended to be optimistic: "In this media-heavy world, it is likely that brains that are more adept at media multitasking will be passed along and these changes will be naturally selected," the report states. "After all, information is power, and if one can process more information all at once, perhaps one can be more powerful." This is techno-social Darwinism, nature red in pixel and claw.

Other experts aren't so sure. As neurologist Jordan Grafman told *Time* magazine: "Kids that are instant messaging while doing homework, playing games online and watching TV, I predict, aren't going to do well in the long run." "I think this generation of kids is guinea pigs," educational psychologist Jane Healy told the *San Francisco Chronicle*; she worries that they might become adults who engage in "very quick but very shallow thinking." Or, as the novelist Walter Kirn suggests in a deft essay in *The Atlantic*, we might be headed for an "Attention-Deficit Recession."

> Noting potential negative effects on children is a good way for Rosen to establish pathos, to make a strong emotional connection with her readers.

Paying Attention

When we talk about multitasking, we are really talking about attention: the art of paying attention, the ability to shift our attention, and, more broadly, to exercise judgment about what objects are worthy of our attention. People who have achieved great things often credit for their success a finely honed skill for paying attention. When asked about his particular genius, Isaac Newton responded that if he had made any discoveries, it was "owing more to patient attention than to any other talent."

Rosen moves toward a conclusion by quoting Newton and James, historical figures whose contributions to culture have been monumental. Each of them, like Lord Chesterfield, recommends paying attention to one thing at a time.

William James, the great psychologist, wrote at length about the varieties of human attention. In *The Principles of Psychology* (1890), he outlined the differences among "sensorial attention," "intellectual attention," "passive attention," and the like, and noted the "gray chaotic indiscriminateness" of the minds of people who were incapable of paying attention. James compared our stream of thought to a river, and his observations presaged the cognitive "bottlenecks" described later by neurologists: "On the whole easy simple flowing predominates in it, the drift of things is with the pull of gravity, and effortless attention is the rule," he wrote. "But at intervals an obstruction, a set-back, a log-jam occurs, stops the current, creates an eddy, and makes things temporarily move the other way."

To James, steady attention was thus the default condition of a mature mind, an ordinary state undone only by perturbation. To readers a century later, that placid portrayal may seem alien—as though depicting a bygone world. Instead, today's multitasking adult may find something more familiar in James's description of the youthful mind: an "extreme mobility of the attention" that "makes the child seem to belong less to himself than to every object which happens to catch his notice." For some people, James noted, this challenge is never overcome; such people only get their work done "in the interstices of their mind-wandering." Like Chesterfield, James believed that the transition from youthful distraction to mature attention was in large part the result of personal mastery and discipline—and so was illustrative of character. "The faculty of voluntarily bringing back a wandering attention, over and over again," he wrote, "is the very root of judgment, character, and will."

Rosen reaches the conclusion that "our collective will to pay attention seems fairly weak," and she has provided a good deal of evidence to support that conclusion.

Today, our collective will to pay attention seems fairly weak. We require advice books to teach us how to avoid distraction. In the not-too-distant future we may even employ new devices to help us overcome the unintended attention deficits created by today's gadgets. As one *New York Times* article recently suggested, "Further research could help create clever technology, like sensors or smart software that workers could instruct with their preferences and priorities to serve as a high tech 'time nanny' to ease the modern multitasker's plight." Perhaps we will all accept as a matter of course a computer governor—like the devices placed on engines so that people can't drive cars beyond a certain speed. Our technological governors might prompt us with reminders to set mental limits when we try to do too much, too quickly, all at once.

Rosen admits that perhaps it's too late to turn back the clock on multitasking and that modern society may need to resign itself to a tradeoff between information and wisdom.

Then again, perhaps we will simply adjust and come to accept what James called "acquired inattention." E-mails pouring in, cell phones ringing, televisions blaring, podcasts streaming—all this may become background noise, like the "din of a foundry or factory" that James observed workers could scarcely avoid at first, but which eventually became just another part of their daily routine. For the younger generation of multitaskers, the great electronic din is an expected part of everyday life. And given what neuroscience and anecdotal evidence have shown us, this state of constant intentional self-distraction could well be of profound detriment to individual and cultural well-being. When people do their work only in the "interstices of their mind-wandering," with crumbs of attention rationed out among many competing tasks, their culture may gain in information, but it will surely weaken in wisdom.

■ GUIDE TO RESPONDING TO THE RHETORICAL SITUATION

Understanding the Rhetorical Situation

When you want to present the results of research you have done, consider composing an investigative report. Such a report commonly has the following features:

- An investigative report defines an issue or phenomenon in precise terms.
- An investigative report makes clear why the issue or phenomenon is one that needs to be investigated.
- An investigative report provides convincing facts and details to help readers understand how the issue or phenomenon affects different groups that have some stake in the situation.
- An investigative report uses direct quotations to vividly convey the perspectives of various groups with a stake in the issue or phenomenon.
- An investigative report clearly identifies the conclusion readers should reach.

The following sections will help you compose an investigative report about the Millennial Generation or another generation that interests you. To work with an online guide to the elements of the rhetorical situation, access your English CourseMate through cengagebrain.com.

Identifying an opportunity

Until you read this chapter, you may not have given much thought to generational labels. Now that you have been considering what it means to be part of a generation, you may be wondering just how accurate and appropriate such labels are. Are they fair ("the greatest") or unfair ("narcissistic")? Are any of them mutually exclusive or overlapping?

As you consider a specific generation, what do you want to know more about? Do you want to investigate the existing label for that generation or find out more about some of its members, their values, accomplishments, and hopes? Maybe you're interested in investigating how generational labels relate to the activities or functions of on-campus offices: the Office of Student Affairs, the Office of Career Services, the Admissions Office, or the Alumni Office. Have you noticed that you are treated differently at any of those offices than a student from another generation? Have older or younger students reported different treatment and expectations from any of those offices? Perhaps you have noticed behaviors, cultural touchstones, or values that are common to a generation but that others have overlooked? Whatever details you have noticed or experiences you have had, you should tap them as you launch your own investigation of generational identity.

1. Make a list of values, behaviors, cultural touchstones, or other characteristics associated with a particular generation. (You might be able to draw

on the writing you've done in response to questions presented earlier in this chapter.) Who do you know who embodies the label of a specific generation? What evidence from that person's life or behavior can you provide that helps support your assertion?

2. Where and when do the various generations of students (or instructors) on campus display their differing characteristics? Which characteristics are immediately identifiable or familiar? Which characteristics are less obvious or unfamiliar? How do you know that someone has those less obvious qualities? Write for a few minutes about these considerations. Be prepared to share your response with the rest of the class.

3. Choose a single characteristic of any generation you would like to explore further, in order to determine its causes and consequences. Write four or five sentences that describe that characteristic and explain how it affects the generation itself or other generations. Be prepared to share your sentences with the rest of the class.

Locating an audience

The following questions will help you identify the rhetorical audience for your investigative report on some characteristic of (or label for) a specific generation. Once you identify an audience who will be interested in or affected by your analysis, you'll be able to choose the best way to deliver your report.

1. List the names of the persons or groups who are affected by or have an interest in the particular generational characteristic (or label) you're going to explore. (This step may require some research.)

2. Next to the name of each potential audience, write reasons that audience could have for acknowledging the significance of this generational characteristic (or label). In other words, what information might convince that audience that an investigation of this particular characteristic (or label) could be important to them?

3. What motivation might each potential audience have for learning more about the generational characteristic (or label)? What emotional response might each audience be expected to have to your investigative report? What logical conclusions might the potential audiences reach about generational labels or mislabels? In what ways might each audience help you confirm or disprove the accuracy of such labels? What actions could these audiences reasonably be expected to take in response to your report?

4. With your audience's interests and motivation in mind, look again at the descriptions of generational characteristics that you composed in the preceding section. Decide which description will enable your audience to feel invested in exploring this particular characteristic (or label) in greater detail in order to understand why and how it affects them. At this point, it will probably be necessary to revise your best description to tailor it to the audiences.

Identifying a fitting response

As you know by now, different purposes and different audiences call for different kinds of texts delivered through different media. For example, realizing that the preferences of an older generation are being overlooked by your school's food services might prompt you to write a flyer and circulate it in the student union, in order to raise awareness of the predominance of fast food on campus and its implications for students' health and satisfaction. Or perhaps discovering that your generation lacks experience in public speaking might lead you to compose and deliver a multimedia presentation to your first-year writing classmates, with the purpose of explaining the curricular opportunities that can help them address this shortcoming. The point is that once you identify your rhetorical opportunity, audience, and purpose, you need to determine what kind of text will best respond to the rhetorical situation.

Use the following questions to help you narrow your purpose and shape your response:

1. What facts and details do you need to provide in order to get your audience to recognize the validity or significance of the specific generational feature (characteristic or label) you are investigating?
2. What are the various (perhaps conflicting) perspectives on this generation that you must acknowledge?
3. Are you asking the audience to adopt a new perspective, or do you want the audience to perform a particular action in response to your writing?
4. What is the best way to reach this audience? That is, to what kind of text is this audience most likely to respond? (Chapter 13 can help you explore options for media and design.)

Writing an Investigative Report: Working with Your Available Means

Shaping your investigative report

Like many other genres, investigative reports take advantage of the power of the rhetorical appeals. While establishing the writer's ethos, the introduction of an investigative report provides readers with a specific description or definition of the issue or phenomenon to be explored as well as the writer's stance concerning that issue. Mark Bauerlein, for example, opens his investigative report with statistics—2,272 texts a month, nine hours of social networking a week—about young people's communication methods. After these descriptive numbers, he identifies the topic of his report: that visible nonverbal behaviors are missing from these communication methods.

pages 64–65, 67–68

The body of an investigative report provides facts, details, and direct quotations that further clarify the issue or phenomenon being examined while shaping the logic (and thus the persuasiveness) of the writer's argument. A successful investigative report is one in which the writer displays good sense in the presentation and analysis of evidence. The writer uses attributive tags to show where each piece of

pages 75–77

evidence came from and to indicate that each source is credible and knowledgable about the topic, thereby enhancing the writer's ethos as well as the report's logos. For example, Bauerlein refers to the research of influential anthropologist Edward Hall, who wrote about the "silent language" as early as 1959. In describing Hall's research on how communication breaks down across cultures, Bauerlein clarifies his purpose: he is applying Hall's cross-cultural communication research findings to instances of miscommunication within a single culture. In particular, Bauerlein is investigating miscommunication that occurs because some participants are less adept at reading nonverbal signals than others. Bauerlein's citations and quotations support his thesis and help build the logos of his argument. If Bauerlein had used video to deliver his report (in the form of a short documentary, for example, or a segment on a news show), he could have shown clips from archived interviews with Hall and presented graphics to illustrate the quantitative research from which he is drawing. Such visual information would further support his credibility.

The body of an investigative report also traces the effects of the issue or phenomenon on various groups. Every use of examples, facts, statistics, and other data builds the ethos of the writer at the same time as it establishes the appeal of logos.

In addition, the body of an investigative report characterizes fairly the positions and motivations of the various groups interested in or affected by the issue or phenomenon, thereby strengthening the writer's ethos and logos. As you can see, all the rhetorical appeals must continually overlap, even if one appeal is emphasized over others at certain points. In a successful investigative report, the writer presents different perspectives in a fair, even-handed way, balancing the ethical appeal of good sense with the logical appeal of supporting information. The writer attends carefully to the connotations of words used to describe the different perspectives of the various groups and gives voice to members of these different groups by quoting them directly.

Finally, the conclusion of an investigative report brings together the various perspectives on the issue or phenomenon and sometimes makes a final appeal

Introduction	Body	Conclusion
▶ Establishes ethos ▶ Describes or defines the issue ▶ States the thesis	▶ Establishes logos ▶ Provides facts, details, and direct quotations ▶ Traces the effects of the issue on various groups	▶ Brings together various perspectives, making an emotional connection ▶ Makes a final attempt to connect with the audience, establishing pathos ▶ Includes a (reasonable) appeal to the audience to adopt a particular attitude or undertake a specific action

for readers to adopt a specific attitude or opinion or take a specific action, using the emotional appeal (of pathos) by connecting the writer's cause with the interests of the readers.

Revision and peer review

After you've drafted a strong version of your investigative report, ask one of your classmates to read it. You'll want your classmate to respond to your work in a way that helps you revise it so that it is the strongest investigative report it can be, one that identifies a rhetorical opportunity, addresses your intended audience, helps you fulfill your purpose, and is delivered in the most appropriate means available to you and your audience.

Questions for a peer reviewer

1. To what opportunity for change is the writer responding?
2. Who might be the writer's intended audience? What might be the writer's purpose? How do audience and purpose come together?
3. What information did you receive from the introduction? Does the writer define the issue or phenomenon in terms that will make sense to the audience? What suggestions do you have for the writer regarding the introduction?
4. Note the writer's thesis statement. If you cannot locate a thesis statement, what thesis statement might work for this report?
5. Note the assertions the writer makes to support the report's thesis. Are the assertions presented in chronological or emphatic order? How does that order enhance the report's overall effectiveness? Which of the assertions might you reorder? Why?
6. If you cannot locate a series of assertions, what assertions could be made to support the thesis? In what order?
7. Mark the supporting ideas (presented using narration, cause-and-consequence analysis, description, exemplification, process analysis, or definition) that the writer offers to support the assertions.
8. What reasons are given for investigating the issue or phenomenon?
9. What facts and details are provided to explain how the issue or phenomenon affects different groups that might have an interest in or connection to it?
10. Whom does the writer quote? What evidence does the writer provide for the credibility of the sources quoted? Whose perspectives are represented in direct quotations? Whose perspectives are not represented through the use of quotations? Can you ascertain why the writer made those decisions?
11. How does the writer establish ethos? How could the writer strengthen this appeal?
12. How does the writer make use of pathos? How exactly does the writer connect his or her cause with the interests of the rhetorical audience?
13. What specific conclusion do you reach about the issue or phenomenon as a result of reading the report?
14. What section of the report did you most enjoy? Least enjoy? Why?

INVESTIGATIVE REPORTS IN THREE MEDIA

Online Report

Ryan Healy's investigation responds to the question "Why Isn't Mainstream Gen Y Buying into the New Web?" in his blog post for *Employee Evolution.* To read it, find *Writing in Three Media* in your English Course-Mate, accessed through cengagebrain.com.

Courtesy Ryan Healy

Video Report

PBS NewsHour filmed a report on the Pew Research Center's study of the Millennials. To view it, find *Writing in Three Media* in your English Course-Mate, accessed through cengagebrain.com.

Courtesy of PBS

Print Report

In the following report, Columbia University student Jenn Mayer investigates what music videos and MTV programming mean to her generation.

Helga Esteb/Shutterstock.com

Jenn could easily have explored her generation's relationship to the music video using any of a variety of genres and media. If her main purpose had been to reflect on the ways in which *Total Request Live* had a formative effect on her, she might have written a memoir to post on her blog. If she had wanted to convince others that the music video is truly the "lasting art form" that she labels it, she could have gathered her evidence into a position argument. But Jenn realized that her extensive research, including interviews with Columbia College classmates, lent itself to an investigative report. And, as a writer for *The Eye*, the weekly magazine affiliated with the *Columbia Daily Spectator* (an undergraduate newspaper), she was able to use that publication to deliver her report to a large audience likely to be interested in the same topic: her college peers who also grew up with *TRL, Pop-Up Video*, Britney Spears, and the Backstreet Boys.

The Last of the Music Videos

a dying art form finds a new home

by Jenn Mayer

Video killed the radio star, but who killed the video?

MTV's *Total Request Live* was canceled late last year after a decade-long run. In a sense, *TRL* defined a generation—ours. In the late '90s and early '00s, scores of tweens would rush home from middle school to see the hottest Britney Spears and Backstreet Boys videos. On the show, pop stars showcased synchronized dance moves and flawless bodies that made teenage girls shriek and cry. While *TRL* was culturally crucial in our younger years, the show's former popularity also indicates how important music videos once were for MTV. The end of the *TRL* era also seemed to symbolize the end of the era of music videos.

The demise of music videos seems clear now that MTV has all but done away with them. In the past, MTV played videos around the clock, providing an additional, visual outlet for artists to expose themselves and for viewers to hear new music. The golden age of the music video began with Michael Jackson's "Thriller" in 1983. When MTV began to credit the directors of music videos in 1992, videos started to take on a cinematic, short-film quality. Video directors like Spike Jonze, F. Gary Gray, and Michel Gondry later went on to direct full-length films.

To help fuel this nascent art form, MTV developed programs like *Making the Video*, which gave viewers a behind-the-scenes look into the creation of a different hit video every episode. VH1, MTV's corporate cousin, had a similar show in *Pop-Up Video*. Videos were almost ubiquitous, the source of iconic images for our generation—who doesn't remember Sisqó's silver hair in the "Thong Song" video or the members of *NSYNC posing as puppets in "Bye Bye Bye"?

Jenn makes clear that the audience for her report is the generation of readers who were middle schoolers from about 1998 to 2003, and she appeals to pathos by identifying herself as part of that generation.

Jenn defines the topic of her investigative report in clear terms: the decline of the music video, a favorite form of media for some Millennials.

Jenn presents details about specific music videos that establish her ethos and support her appeal to pathos.

Just as the quasi-innocent image of Britney Spears in her "...Baby One More Time" schoolgirl outfit has been replaced in our minds with the image of a shaved head and umbrella, MTV has replaced music videos with reality programming, a field it pioneered with *The Real World*. Now that reality shows dominate prime time, MTV has expanded its offerings to include a slew of dating shows, competitions, and forays into celebrity lifestyles. To remain relevant, it seems as though MTV has been forced to alter its original design to match other major networks.

She presents evidence that the growing popularity of reality shows was the main cause for the decline of music videos.

In addition to MTV's reality programming, YouTube has also contributed to putting the nail in the video coffin. On the site, music videos with A-list directors and multi-million dollar budgets mingle equally with fan-made videos. As Henry Jones, SEAS [School of Engineering and Applied Science] '12, says, "If there's a song I really like, I'll search to see if there's a video. But I don't go on YouTube exclusively to watch multiple videos. It just doesn't seem logical anymore to sit down and actively watch a music video."

This shift away from music videos is also a signal of major change for the music industry. Illegal file-sharing and waning CD sales have crippled the industry, forcing it to adapt in order to stay afloat. But while stories like the lawsuits against college students who download illegally and the closing of the Virgin Megastore have consistently made headlines, it seems as though music videos have more or less disappeared silently from the airwaves.

Jenn identifies the significance of the decline in music video programming.

But, as Jones suggests, while many people don't search deliberately for music videos, they are directed to them by links or friends' suggestions. This type of viral marketing represents how popular culture continues to embrace music videos, despite their ousting from television. Videos for songs such as MGMT's "Electric Feel" gained popularity through word of mouth, and everyone had seen Beyoncé's "Single Ladies" video even before it was parodied on *Saturday Night Live.* •

Jenn's references to specific artists and songs further supports her appeal to pathos.

Furthermore, the original concept of the music video as an additional link to the artist continues to attract viewers. Emma Gillespie, CC [Columbia College] '09, tunes into videos both online and through MTV sister channels that have continued to show videos, like MTV Jams and MTV Hits. "Videos put a story with the music, and it's fun to see what the artist's interpretation of the song is," she says.

Although MTV has abandoned music videos on its main channel, it does make over 16,000 videos available for online streaming. Britney Spears' "Circus" video, which marked her highly publicized comeback, boasts over 2 million MTV views. One of the many YouTube versions of the same video reports almost 25 million.

Though the music video is not fully dead, it has begun to take on the qualities of a has-been pop star. While today's tweens may not have the same relationship to music videos as teens in the '80s or the TRL generation did, the simple fact is that people continue to invest time in watching them. Rather than lamenting the days when music videos ruled the airwaves, we can rejoice in the medium's status as a lasting art form. Music videos will continue to garner attention and inspire parody for years to come.

Alternatives to the Investigative Report

Fitting responses come in many forms, not just reports. Your instructor might call upon you to consider one of the following opportunities for writing.

1. As you read in the introduction to this chapter, generational labels are generalizations about specific groups with which some people may not agree. Compose an essay that defines your generation in a fresh way. What name would you give your generation? What characterizes your generation? What differentiates it from and connects it to other generations? pages 64–66

pages 73–74

2. Compose a narrative about a day in the life of a fellow student from a generation other than your own. Describe in vivid detail how and where your campus accommodates—or does not accommodate—someone from that generation. You will probably need to do library or online research and/or conduct interviews to fulfill this assignment.

3. Identify a particular problem on your campus that results from lack of attention to a specific generational characteristic (of your generation or another). Write a proposal that describes the problem and argues for a particular practical solution. As you write, make sure to consider your audience (whose members should be in a position to help implement your solution) and the feasibility of your proposal (its cost and how it might affect the institution's research, teaching, and service missions).

Julia Angwin

Julia Angwin was raised in Silicon Valley by parents who worked in technology and considers herself a "digital native." Angwin began her career as a journalist for The Washington Post *and also has experience working for the* San Francisco Chronicle. *In 2000, she began working for the* Wall Street Journal *as a technology editor, writing a column called "The Decoder." In 2009 she authored* Stealing MySpace, *a book that describes the history of the first successful social networking site.*

In the selection that follows, Angwin analyzes the "increasingly public" nature of Facebook friendships and suggests that members of these social media sites need to reconsider how they are used.

How Facebook is Making Friending Obsolete *(2009)*

"Friending" wasn't used as a verb until about five years ago, when social networks such as Friendster, MySpace and Facebook burst onto the scene.

Suddenly, our friends were something even better—an audience. If blogging felt like shouting into the void, posting updates on a social network felt more like an intimate conversation among friends at a pub.

Inevitably, as our list of friends grew to encompass acquaintances, friends of friends and the girl who sat behind us in seventh-grade homeroom, online friendships became devalued.

Suddenly, we knew as much about the lives of our distant acquaintances as we did about the lives of our intimates—what they'd had for dinner, how they felt about Tiger Woods and so on.

Enter Twitter with a solution: no friends, just followers. These one-way relationships were easier to manage—no more annoying decisions about whether to give your ex-boyfriend access to your photos, no more fussing over who could see your employment and contact information.

Twitter's updates were also easily searchable on the Web, forcing users to be somewhat thoughtful about their posts. The intimate conversation became a talent show, a challenge to prove your intellectual prowess in 140 characters or less.

This fall, Twitter turned its popularity into dollars, inking lucrative deals to allow its users' tweets to be broadcast via search algorithms on Google and Bing.

Soon, Facebook followed suit with deals to distribute certain real-time data to Google and Bing. (Recall that despite being the fifth-most-popular

Web site in the world, Facebook is barely profitable.) Facebook spokesman Barry Schnitt says no money changed hands in the deals but says there was "probably an exchange of value."

Just one catch: Facebook had just "exchanged" to Google and Microsoft something that didn't exist.

10   The vast majority of Facebook users restrict updates to their friends, and do not expect those updates to appear in public search results. (In fact, many people restrict their Facebook profile from appearing at all in search results.)

So Facebook had little content to provide to Google's and Bing's real-time search results. When Google's real-time search launched earlier this month, its results were primarily filled with Twitter updates.

Coincidentally, Facebook presented its 350 million members with a new default privacy setting last week. For most people, the new suggested settings would open their Facebook updates and information to the entire world. Mr. Schnitt says the new privacy suggestions are an acknowledgement of "the way we think the world is going."

Facebook Chief Executive Mark Zuckerberg led by example, opening up his previously closed profile, including goofy photos of himself curled up with a teddy bear.

Facebook also made public formerly private info such as profile pictures, gender, current city and the friends list. (Mr. Schnitt suggests that users are free to lie about their hometown or take down their profile picture to protect their privacy; in response to users' complaints, the friends list can now be restricted to be viewed only by friends.)

15   Of course, many people will reject the default settings on Facebook and keep on chatting with only their Facebook friends. (Mr. Schnitt said more than 50% of its users had rejected the defaults at last tally.)

But those who want a private experience on Facebook will have to work harder at it: if you inadvertently post a comment on a friend's profile page that has been opened to the public, your comment will be public too.

Just as Facebook turned friends into a commodity, it has likewise gathered our personal data—our updates, our baby photos, our endless chirping birthday notes—and readied it to be bundled and sold.

So I give up. Rather than fighting to keep my Facebook profile private, I plan to open it up to the public—removing the fiction of intimacy and friendship.

But I will also remove the vestiges of my private life from Facebook and make sure I never post anything that I wouldn't want my parents, employer, next-door neighbor or future employer to see. You'd be smart to do the same.

20   We'll need to treat this increasingly public version of Facebook with the same hard-headedness that we treat Twitter: as a place to broadcast, but not a place for vulnerability. A place to carefully calibrate, sanitize and bowdlerize our words for every possible audience, now and forever. Not a place for intimacy with friends.

NICHOLAS CARR

Nicholas Carr (1959–) writes primarily about interactions between culture, technology, and economics. He has written numerous articles for influential magazines both in America and Europe, with articles or columns in The Guardian *in* London, The Atlantic, *the* New York Times, *the* Wall Street Journal, *and* Wired *just to name a few. He is also the author of* The Shallows: What the Internet Is Doing to Our Brains *(2010),* The Big Switch: Rewiring the World, from Edison to Google *(2008), and* Does It Matter *(2004)? Carr lectures and speaks on a variety of subjects and maintains a blog titled Rough Type.*

Is Google Making Us Stupid? *(2008)*

"Dave, stop. Stop, will you? Stop, Dave. Will you stop, Dave?" So the supercomputer HAL pleads with the implacable astronaut Dave Bowman in a famous and weirdly poignant scene toward the end of Stanley Kubrick's *2001: A Space Odyssey.* Bowman, having nearly been sent to a deep-space death by the malfunctioning machine, is calmly, coldly disconnecting the memory circuits that control its artificial "brain." "Dave, my mind is going," HAL says, forlornly. "I can feel it. I can feel it."

I can feel it, too. Over the past few years I've had an uncomfortable sense that someone, or something, has been tinkering with my brain, remapping the neural circuitry, reprogramming the memory. My mind isn't going—so far as I can tell—but it's changing. I'm not thinking the way I used to think. I can feel it most strongly when I'm reading. Immersing myself in a book or a lengthy article used to be easy. My mind would get caught up in the narrative or the turns of the argument, and I'd spend hours strolling through long stretches of prose. That's rarely the case anymore. Now my concentration often starts to drift after two or three pages. I get fidgety, lose the thread, begin looking for something else to do. I feel as if I'm always dragging my wayward brain back to the text. The deep reading that used to come naturally has become a struggle.

I think I know what's going on. For more than a decade now, I've been spending a lot of time online, searching and surfing and sometimes adding to the great databases of the Internet. The Web has been a godsend to me as a writer. Research that once required days in the stacks or periodical rooms of libraries can now be done in minutes. A few Google searches, some quick clicks on hyperlinks, and I've got the telltale fact or pithy quote I was after. Even when I'm not working, I'm as likely as not to be foraging in the Web's info-thickets' reading and writing e-mails, scanning headlines and blog posts, watching videos and listening to podcasts, or just tripping from link to link to link. (Unlike footnotes, to which they're sometimes likened, hyperlinks don't merely point to related works; they propel you toward them.)

For me, as for others, the Net is becoming a universal medium, the conduit for most of the information that flows through my eyes and ears and into my mind. The advantages of having immediate access to such an incredibly rich store of information are many, and they've been widely described and duly applauded. "The perfect recall of silicon memory," *Wired's* Clive Thompson has written, "can be an enormous boon to thinking." But that boon comes at a price. As the media theorist Marshall McLuhan pointed out in the 1960s, media are not just passive channels of information. They supply the stuff of thought, but they also shape the process of thought. And what the Net seems to be doing is chipping away my capacity for concentration and contemplation. My mind now expects to take in information the way the Net distributes it: in a swiftly moving stream of particles. Once I was a scuba diver in the sea of words. Now I zip along the surface like a guy on a Jet Ski.

5   I'm not the only one. When I mention my troubles with reading to friends and acquaintances—literary types, most of them—many say they're having similar experiences. The more they use the Web, the more they have to fight to stay focused on long pieces of writing. Some of the bloggers I follow have also begun mentioning the phenomenon. Scott Karp, who writes a blog about online media, recently confessed that he has stopped reading books altogether. "I was a lit major in college, and used to be [a] voracious book reader," he wrote. "What happened?" He speculates on the answer: "What if I do all my reading on the web not so much because the way I read has changed, i.e. I'm just seeking convenience, but because the way I THINK has changed?"

Bruce Friedman, who blogs regularly about the use of computers in medicine, also has described how the Internet has altered his mental habits. "I now have almost totally lost the ability to read and absorb a longish article on the web or in print," he wrote earlier this year. A pathologist who has long been on the faculty of the University of Michigan Medical School, Friedman elaborated on his comment in a telephone conversation with me. His thinking, he said, has taken on a "staccato" quality, reflecting the way he quickly scans short passages of text from many sources online. "I can't read *War and Peace* anymore," he admitted. "I've lost the ability to do that. Even a blog post of more than three or four paragraphs is too much to absorb. I skim it."

Anecdotes alone don't prove much. And we still await the long-term neurological and psychological experiments that will provide a definitive picture of how Internet use affects cognition. But a recently published study of online research habits, conducted by scholars from University College London, suggests that we may well be in the midst of a sea change in the way we read and think. As part of the five-year research program, the scholars examined computer logs documenting the behavior of visitors to two popular research sites, one operated by the British Library and one by a U.K. educational consortium, that provide access to journal articles, e-books, and other sources of written information. They found that people using the sites exhibited "a form of skimming activity," hopping from one source to another and rarely returning to any source they'd already visited. They typically read no more than one or two pages of an article or book before they would "bounce" out to another site. Sometimes they'd save a long article, but there's no evidence that they ever went back and actually read it. The authors of the study report:

> It is clear that users are not reading online in the traditional sense; indeed there are signs that new forms of "reading" are emerging as users "power browse" horizontally through titles, contents pages and abstracts going for quick wins. It almost seems that they go online to avoid reading in the traditional sense.

Thanks to the ubiquity of text on the Internet, not to mention the popularity of text-messaging on cell phones, we may well be reading more today than we did in the 1970s or 1980s, when television was our medium of choice. But it's a different kind of reading, and behind it lies a different kind of thinking—perhaps even a new sense of the self. "We are not only what we read," says Maryanne Wolf, a developmental psychologist at Tufts University and the author of *Proust and the Squid: The Story and Science of the Reading Brain.* "We are how we read." Wolf worries that the style of reading promoted by the Net, a style that puts "efficiency" and "immediacy" above all else, may be weakening our capacity for the kind of deep reading that emerged when an earlier technology, the printing press, made long and complex works of prose commonplace. When we read online, she says, we tend to become "mere decoders of information." Our ability to interpret text, to make the rich mental connections that form when we read deeply and without distraction, remains largely disengaged.

Reading, explains Wolf, is not an instinctive skill for human beings. It's 10 not etched into our genes the way speech is. We have to teach our minds how to translate the symbolic characters we see into the language we understand. And the media or other technologies we use in learning and practicing the craft of reading play an important part in shaping the neural circuits inside our brains. Experiments demonstrate that readers of ideograms, such as the Chinese, develop a mental circuitry for reading that is very different from the circuitry found in those of us whose written language employs an alphabet. The variations extend across many regions of the brain, including those that govern such essential cognitive functions as memory and the interpretation of visual and auditory stimuli. We can expect as well that the circuits woven by our use of the Net will be different from those woven by our reading of books and other printed works.

Sometime in 1882, Friedrich Nietzsche bought a typewriter—a Malling-Hansen Writing Ball, to be precise. His vision was failing, and keeping his eyes focused on a pag had become exhausting and painful, often bringing on crushing headaches. He had been forced to curtail his writing, and he feared that he would soon have to give it up. The typewriter rescued him, at least for a time. Once he had mastered touch-typing, he was able to write with his eyes closed, using only the tips of his fingers. Words could once again flow from his mind to the page.

But the machine had a subtler effect on his work. One of Nietzsche's friends, a composer, noticed a change in the style of his writing. His already terse prose had become even tighter, more telegraphic. "Perhaps you will through this instrument even take to a new idiom," the friend wrote in a letter, noting that, in his own work, his "'thoughts' in music and language often depend on the quality of pen and paper."

"You are right," Nietzsche replied, "our writing equipment takes part in the forming of our thoughts." Under the sway of the machine, writes the German media scholar Friedrich A. Kittler, Nietzsche's prose "changed from arguments to aphorisms, from thoughts to puns, from rhetoric to telegram style."

The human brain is almost infmitely malleable. People used to think that our mental meshwork, the dense connections formed among the 100 billion or so neurons inside our skulls, was largely fixed by the time we reached adulthood. But brain researchers have discovered that that's not the case. James Olds, a professor of neuroscience who directs the Krasnow Institute for Advanced Study at George Mason University, says that even the adult mind "is very plastic." Nerve cells routinely break old connections and form new ones. "The brain," according to Olds, "has the ability to reprogram itself on the fly, altering the way it functions."

15   As we use what the sociologist Daniel Bell has called our "intellectual technologies"—the tools that extend our mental rather than our physical capacities—we inevitably begin to take on the qualities of those technologies. The mechanical clock, which came into common use in the 14th century, provides a compelling example. In *Technics and Civilization*, the historian and cultural critic Lewis Mumford described how the clock "disassociated time from human events and helped create the belief in an independent world of mathematically measurable sequences." The "abstract framework of divided time" became "the point of reference for both action and thought."

The clock's methodical ticking helped bring into being the scientific mind and the scientific man. But it also took something away. As the late MIT computer scientist Joseph Weizenbaum observed in his 1976 book, *Computer Power and Human Reason: From Judgment to Calculation,* the conception of the world that emerged from the widespread use of timekeeping instruments "remains an impoverished version of the older one, for it rests on a rejection of those direct experiences that formed the basis for, and indeed constituted, the old reality." In deciding when to eat, to work, to sleep, to rise, we stopped listening to our senses and started obeying the clock.

The process of adapting to new intellectual technologies is reflected in the changing metaphors we use to explain ourselves to ourselves. When the mechanical clock arrived, people began thinking of their brains as operating "like clockwork." Today, in the age of software, we have come to think of them as operating "like computers." But the changes, neuroscience tells us, go much deeper than metaphor. Thanks to our brain's plasticity, the adaptation occurs also at a biological level.

The Internet promises to have particularly far-reaching effects on cognition. In a paper published in 1936, the British mathematician Alan Turing proved that a digital computer, which at the time existed only as a theoretical machine, could be programmed to perform the function of any other information-processing device. And that's what we're seeing today. The Internet, an immeasurably powerful computing system, is subsuming most of our other intellectual technologies. It's becoming our map and our clock, our printing press and our typewriter, our calculator and our telephone, and our radio and TV.

When the Net absorbs a medium, that medium is re-created in the Net's image. It injects the medium's content with hyperlinks, blinking ads, and other digital gewgaws, and it surrounds the content with the content of all the other media it has absorbed. A new email message, for instance, may announce its arrival as we're glancing over the latest headlines at a newspaper's site. The result is to scatter our attention and diffuse our concentration.

The Net's influence doesn't end at the edges of a computer screen, either. As people's minds become attuned to the crazy quilt of Internet media, traditional media have to adapt to the audience's new expectations. Television programs add text crawls and pop-up ads, and magazines and newspapers shorten their articles, introduce capsule summaries, and crowd their pages with easy-to-browse info-snippets. When, in March of this year, *The New York Times* decided to devote the second and third pages of every edition to article abstracts, its design director, Tom Bodkin, explained that the "shortcuts" would give harried readers a quick "taste" of the day's news, sparing them the "less efficient" method of actually turning the pages and reading the articles. Old media have little choice but to play by the new-media rules. 20

Never has a communications system played so many roles in our lives—or exerted such broad influence over our thoughts—as the Internet does today. Yet, for all that's been written about the Net, there's been little consideration of how, exactly, it's reprogramming us. The Net's intellectual ethic remains obscure.

About the same time that Nietzsche started using his typewriter, an earnest young man named Frederick Winslow Taylor carried a stopwatch into the Midvale Steel plant in Philadelphia and began a historic series of experiments aimed at improving the efficiency of the plant's machinists. With the approval of Midvale's owners, he recruited a group of factory hands, set them to work on various metalworking machines, and recorded and timed their every movement as well as the operations of the machines. By breaking down every job into a sequence of small, discrete steps and then testing different ways of performing each one, Taylor created a set of precise instructions— an "algorithm," we might say today—for how each worker should work. Midvale's employees grumbled about the strict new regime, claiming that it turned them into little more than automatons, but the factory's productivity soared.

More than a hundred years after the invention of the steam engine, the Industrial Revolution had at last found its philosophy and its philosopher. Taylor's tight industrial choreography—his "system," as he liked to call it— was embraced by manufacturers throughout the country and, in time, around the world. Seeking maximum speed, maximum efficiency, and maximum output, factory owners used time-and-motion studies to organize their work and configure the jobs of their workers. The goal, as Taylor defined it in his celebrated 1911 treatise, *The Principles of Scientific Management,* was to identify and adopt, for every job, the "one best method" of work and thereby to effect "the gradual substitution of science for rule of thumb throughout the mechanic arts." Once his system was applied to all acts of manual labor, Taylor assured his followers, it would bring about a restructuring not only of industry but of society, creating a utopia of perfect efficiency. "In the past the man has been first," he declared; "in the future the system must be first."

Taylor's system is still very much with us; it remains the ethic of industrial manufacturing. And now, thanks to the growing power that computer engineers and software coders wield over our intellectual lives, Taylor's ethic is beginning to govern the realm of the mind as well. The Internet is a machine designed for the efficient and automated collection, transmission, and manipulation of information, and its legions of programmers are intent on finding the "one best method"—the perfect algorithm—to carry out every mental movement of what we've come to describe as "knowledge work."

25   Google's headquarters, in Mountain View, California—the Googleplex—is the Internet's high church, and the religion practiced inside its walls is Taylorism. Google, says its chief executive, Eric Schmidt, is "a company that's founded around the science of measurement," and it is striving to "systematize everything" it does. Drawing on the terabytes of behavioral data it collects through its search engine and other sites, it carries out thousands of experiments a day, according to the *Harvard Business Review*, and it uses the results to refine the algorithms that increasingly control how people find information and extract meaning from it. What Taylor did for the work of the hand, Google is doing for the work of the mind.

The company has declared that its mission is "to organize the world's information and make it universally accessible and useful." It seeks to develop "the perfect search engine," which it defines as something that "understands exactly what you mean and gives you back exactly what you want." In Google's view, information is a kind of commodity, a utilitarian resource that can be mined and processed with industrial efficiency. The more pieces of information we can "access" and the faster we can extract their gist, the more productive we become as thinkers.

Where does it end? Sergey Brin and Larry Page, the gifted young men who founded Google while pursuing doctoral degrees in computer science at Stanford, speak frequently of their desire to turn their search engine into an artificial intelligence, a HAL-like machine that might be connected directly to our brains. "The ultimate search engine is something as smart as people—or smarter," Page said in a speech a few years back. "For us, working on search is a way to work on artificial intelligence." In a 2004 interview with *Newsweek*, Brin said, "Certainly if you had all the world's information directly attached to your brain, or an artificial brain that was smarter than your brain, you'd be better off." Last year, Page told a convention of scientists that Google is "really trying to build artificial intelligence and to do it on a large scale."

Such an ambition is a natural one, even an admirable one, for a pair of math whizzes with vast quantities of cash at their disposal and a small army of computer scientists in their employ. A fundamentally scientific enterprise, Google is motivated by a desire to use technology, in Eric Schmidt's words, "to solve problems that have never been solved before," and artificial intelligence is the hardest problem out there. Why wouldn't Brin and Page want to be the ones to crack it?

Still, their easy assumption that we'd all "be better off" if our brains were supplemented, or even replaced, by an artificial intelligence is unsettling. It suggests a belief that intelligence is the output of a mechanical process, a series of discrete steps that can be isolated, measured, and optimized. In Google's world, the world we enter when we go online, there's little place for the fuzziness of contemplation. Ambiguity is not an opening for insight but a bug to be fixed. The human brain is just an outdated computer that needs a faster processor and a bigger hard drive.

The idea that our minds should operate as high-speed data-processing machines is not only built into the workings of the Internet, it is the network's reigning business model as well. The faster we surf across the Web—the more links we click and pages we view—the more opportunities Google and other companies gain to collect information about us and to feed us advertisements. Most of the proprietors of the commercial Internet have a financial stake in collecting the crumbs of data we leave behind as we flit from link to link—the more crumbs, the better. The last thing these companies want is to encourage leisurely reading or slow, concentrated thought. It's in their economic interest to drive us to distraction.

Maybe I'm just a worrywart. Just as there's a tendency to glorify technological progress, there's a countertendency to expect the worst of every new tool or machine. In Plato's Phaedrus, Socrates bemoaned the development of writing. He feared that, as people came to rely on the written word as a substitute for the knowledge they used to carry inside their heads, they would, in the words of one of the dialogue's characters, "cease to exercise their memory and become forgetful." And because they would be able to "receive a quantity of information without proper instruction," they would "be thought very knowledgeable when they are for the most part quite ignorant." They would be "filled with the conceit of wisdom instead of real wisdom." Socrates wasn't wrong—the new technology did often have the effects he feared—but he was shortsighted. He couldn't foresee the many ways that writing and reading would serve to spread information, spur fresh ideas, and expand human knowledge (if not wisdom).

The arrival of Gutenberg's printing press, in the 15th century, set off another round of teeth gnashing. The Italian humanist Hieronimo Squarciafico worried that the easy availability of books would lead to intellectual laziness, making men "less studious" and weakening their minds. Others argued that cheaply printed books and broadsheets would undermine religious authority, demean the work of scholars and scribes, and spread sedition and debauchery. As New York University professor Clay Shirky notes, "Most of the arguments made against the printing press were correct, even prescient." But, again, the doomsayers were unable to imagine the myriad blessings that the printed word would deliver.

So, yes, you should be skeptical of my skepticism. Perhaps those who dismiss critics of the Internet as Luddites or nostalgists will be proved correct, and from our hyperactive, data-stoked minds will spring a golden age of intellectual

30

discovery and universal wisdom. Then again, the Net isn't the alphabet, and although it may replace the printing press, it produces something altogether different. The kind of deep reading that a sequence of printed pages promotes is valuable not just for the knowledge we acquire from the author's words but for the intellectual vibrations those words set off within our own minds. In the quiet spaces opened up by the sustained, undistracted reading of a book, or by any other act of contemplation, for that matter, we make our own associations, draw our own inferences and analogies, foster our own ideas. Deep reading, as Maryanne Wolf argues, is indistinguishable from deep thinking.

If we lose those quiet spaces, or fill them up with "content," we will sacrifice something important not only in our selves but in our culture. In a recent essay, the playwright Richard Foreman eloquently described what's at stake:

35   I come from a tradition of Western culture, in which the ideal (my ideal) was the complex, dense and "cathedral-like" structure of the highly educated and articulate personality—a man or woman who carried inside themselves a personally constructed and unique version of the entire heritage of the West. [But now] I see within us all (myself included) the replacement of complex inner density with a new kind of self-evolving under the pressure of information overload and the technology of the "instantly available."

As we are drained of our "inner repertory of dense cultural inheritance," Foreman concluded, we risk turning into "'pancake people'—spread wide and thin as we connect with that vast network of information accessed by the mere touch of a button."

I'm haunted by that scene in *2001*. What makes it so poignant, and so weird, is the computer's emotional response to the disassembly of its mind: its despair as one circuit after another goes dark, its childlike pleading with the astronaut—"I can feel it. I can feel it. I'm afraid"—and its final reversion to what can only be called a state of innocence. HAL's outpouring of feeling contrasts with the emotionlessness that characterizes the human figures in the film, who go about their business with an almost robotic efficiency. Their thoughts and actions feel scripted, as if they're following the steps of an algorithm. In the world of *2001*, people have become so machinelike that the most human character turns out to be a machine. That's the essence of Kubrick's dark prophecy: as we come to rely on computers to mediate our understanding of the world, it is our own intelligence that flattens into artificial intelligence.

A

A Gesture Life (Lee) 83
Abley, Mark 91
Abu Ghraib 89
Achievement Gap in US Education,
    The: Canaries in the Mine
    (Singham) 120
African Americans 57
    civil rights movement of 57
Alcalá, Rafael and Maria
    photographs
Ali, Annas 35-36
Allan, Tony 40
Allende, Isabel 102-106
Allende, Salvador 105
Amado, Jorge 105
Amazon River
    photographs
American Psychological Association.
    See APA
Amphetamines 40
analogies 80
Andalusia, Spain
    photographs
anxiety.
    See communication apprehension
anxious/ambivalent attachment style
    48
APA (American Psychological
    Association)
    See also Publication Manual of the
    American Psychological
    Association
appeals.
    See ethos
    See ethos

logos
    See ethos
logos
    pathos
    See ethos
logos
    pathos
    rhetorical appeals
Aran Islands
    photographs
argument 136
artwork.
    See image(s)
ASL.
    See American Sign Language (ASL)
aspect, of verb
    See also tense
Astoria, Oregon
    photographs
attachment styles 46-48
attributive tags 136-137
audience 135
    locating 135
Autobiography of Malcolm X, The 70

B

Baby Boomers 110, 111, 112
Bagan
    photographs
Bai, Dilli
    photographs
Bangkok, Thailand
    photographs
Bangla Town 35
Bangladesh 35
Battle of Fair Oaks

photographs
Bauerlein, Mark 125, 126-127, 136, 137
Beatles 59
Beauvilain, Christophe 39
Beloit College Mindset List 108, 109, 111
blog(s).
    See also specific blogs
Blue Book 35
body 136-137
    of investigative report 136-137
body images 55
Book of Kells
    photographs
Borges, Jorge Luis 105
Bowlby, John 46
Brazilian Amazon.
    See Amazon Basin
Brothers Grimm Museum
    photographs
BRS.
    See Bibliographic Retrieval Service (BRS)
Buon Ma Thuot, Vietnam
    photographs
Burma
    See also Myanmar

C

Carnegie, Dale 50
Carter, Henry.
    See Leslie, Frank
Carter, Steve 40
Casa Benigna
    photographs

cause-and-effect (cause-andconsequence) analysis 124, 130
Chicago Manual of Style, The
    See CMS
City or the Square Mile 39
civil rights movement 57
claim
    See also thesis statement
classification and division 129
climate communication
    see also interpersonal communication
clothing 49
    femininity in 49
Cobb, Jodi 31
Coffee taste testers
    photographs
Cole, Tim 48
colors of love
    Figure
Columbia Daily Spectator 139
commitment 58
    to self-change 58
communication
    continuum of
        Figure
    mass
        (see also mass media)
    public
        (see also public speaking)
    symbolic activities
        (see also symbols)
    values
        (See also values)
    see also meaning

comparison 48
    social 48
conclusion 137-138
    of investigative report 137-138
conjunction(s)
    See also coordinating conjunction
context 61-62
    for self-change 61-62
continuum of communication
    Figure
Coon Creek, Wisconsin
    photographs
Cordova, Ximena 39-40
Costa Brava, Spain
    photographs
Craig, Carmen
    photographs
credibility
    see also specific types
cross-cultural communication
    see also culture
culture. 51, 54-56, 57
    femininity and 57
    gender in 14
    personal identity and 51, 54-56
    See also organizational culture
    See also organizational culture
    individual names of ethnic groups

D

Dance drugs 40
Daughter of Fortune (Allende) 103
definition 129, 136, 142
delivery.
    guidelines for
        Table

See also public speaking
description 136
    in investigative report 136
development.
    See rhetorical methods of
        development
direct definition 45, 48
DIRS.
    See Dialog Information Retrieval
        Service (DIRS)
discrimination 54-55, 55, 57
    gender 55
    personal identity and 54-55
    sexual orientation 12, 57
dismissive attachment style 47
Disney, Walt 59
domestic abuse.
    See abuse
dress.
    See clothing
Driving Miss Daisy 77
Dumbest Generation, The: How the
    Digital Age Stupefies Young
    Americans and Jeopardizes Our
    Future (Or, Don't Trust Anyone
    Under 30) (Bauerlein) 125
Dun Aengus Celtic Fort
    photographs
dysfunctional communication.
    See egocentric communication

E

Ecstasy 40
editing.
    See also revision
education 51

opportunity for 51
ego boundaries 52
electronic communication 123-124
Elite Model Look competition
     photographs
Ellis, Albert 62
Employee Evolution (blog) 139
English language 68-106, 100-101
Erdrich, Louise 105
ethnicity 68
ethnicity.
     See race
ethos 137
     in investigative report 137
     see also credibility
Eva Luna (Allende) 103
Evans, Joanne 36
     photographs
examples.
     See exemplification
exemplification 129, 137
Extreme Makeover (TV program) 50
Eye, The 139

F

facts 136, 137
Fallarme, David 124-125
families 45, 46-48, 48
     attachment styles of 46-48
     direct definition 45, 48
     identity scripts in 3
     personal identity influence of 2, 3-5
fearful attachment style 46-47
feelings.
     See also emotional display
femininity 49, 57

culture and 57
     in clothing 49
Fendrich, Laurie 127-128
field research (fieldwork).
     See also naturalistic study
fitting response 129-130, 136
     identifying 136
     investigative report as 129-130
Food crisis.
     See Global food crisis
Foran, Charles 90-94
Ford, Kathryn 37
     photographs
foreign-language speakers 94-102
Fortress of the Christian Monarchs
     photographs
Fortress of the Christian Monarchs,
     Córdoba
     photographs
Frey, William H. 94-102
friendships
     see also personal relationships

G

Gandhi, Mohandas 108
gender. 49, 54-55, 55, 56, 57
     discrimination 55
     in culture 57
     peers and 49
     personal identity by 54-55
     race and 56
     socioeconomic class and 13
     See also femininity
     See also femininity
     masculinity, men
     See also femininity

masculinity, men
women
generalizations 54-56
of "other," 54-56
Generation X 110, 111
Generation Y 108, 111
Generation Z 111
generations, labels for 110-111, 112-113
genre
See also names of specific genres
GHB 40
goals 59-60
for self-change 59-60
Gobey, Carl 40
God vs. Darwin: The War Between Evolution and Creationism in the Classroom (Singham) 120
Gombad-e-Qubues, Iran
photographs
Greatest Generation 110, 111, 112

H
Hall, Edward 137
Harrow School
photographs
Haryana, India
photographs
health 50
Healy, Ryan 139
heterosexuality 45
homosexuality 45, 56, 57
discrimination against 57
homophobia 56
Hoover, Eric 113
How to Stubbornly Refuse to Make Yourself Miserable About Anything—Yes, Anything (Ellis) 62
How to Win Friends and Influence People (Carnegie) 50

I
identity scripts 46
Ifuago Province, Philippines
photographs
India 50
individualism 57
infants, development of 52
InfoTrac
Figure
internalization, of others' perspectives 52-56
Internet Generation 111
introduction 136
of investigative report 136
investigative reports 109, 129-130, 134, 136-138, 142-143
alternatives to 142-143
as fitting response 129-130
characteristics of 134
shaping 136-138
Irrigation ditch
photographs
Itaquai River
photographs
Izumo Shinto shrine
photographs

J
Johnson, Samuel 32
Jordan, Michael 59
Jumeirah Beach Residence

photographs
justice 51

K

Kennedy, John F. 108
Kennedy, Robert F. 108
King, Martin Luther, Jr. 108
Knock Down Ginger 35

L

labels 51
Lagos, Marisa 108
Lake Balaton, Hungary
    photographs
Lakoff, Robin Tolmach 87-90
language 68-106
Language and Women's Place (Lakoff)
    87
language.
    See also American Sign Language
    (ASL)
    See also American Sign Language
    (ASL)
    women
leadership.
    See also specific types
Lee, Chang-Rae 83-86
Lee, Lois
    photographs
Leets, Laura 48
legal system 51
Lennon, John 108
lesbians, domestic responsibilities with
    see also homosexuality
Little, Richard 70
Llosa, Mario Vargas 105

logos 137
    in investigative report 137
London 31-42, 35-36, 36, 39, 40
    ethnic population of 35-36, 39
    homosexuals in 40
    illegal drug factories in 10
    interracial relationships in 36, 9
    migrants in 9
    restaurants in 10-11
looking-glass self 53
Lorenz, Konrad 88
Lost Generation 110

M

MacLaine, Shirley 78
MacLeod, Bannatyne
    photographs
Macy, R. H. 59
Malcolm X 108
Marketing Student, The (blog) 124
marriage 57
    same-sex 57
mass media.
    media continuum
        Figure
    See also mass media
    See also mass media
    media literacy
    See also mass media
    media literacy
    social media
Mayer, Jenn 139-142
McBride, Tom 108
media. 50
    continuum
        Figure

influence of 50
See also mass media
See also mass media
media literacy
See also mass media
media literacy
social media
men 57
socialized role of 57
Men's Health 50
Millennial Generation 108-109, 111
MLA (Modern Language Association)
See also MLA Handbook for Writers
of Research Papers, The
Mocuba, Mozambique, Africa
photographs
Modern Language Association.
See MLA
Monk robes
photographs
Morrison, Toni 105
multimedia composition(s).
See also blog(s)
See also blog(s)
podcast(s)
See also blog(s)
podcast(s)
website(s)
See also blog(s)
podcast(s)
website(s)
wiki(s)
multimodal composition(s).
See multimedia composition(s)
Munoz, Manuel 70-75
Myanmar

See also Irrawaddy River
Márquez, García 105

N

narrative 143
Native Speaker (Lee) 83
New Atlantic, The: A Journal of
Technology & Society 130
Nief, Ron 108

O

Ocean food chain
photographs
Of Love and Shadows (Allende) 103
opportunity.
See rhetorical opportunity
orientation
see also sexual orientation

P

Pakistan 35
Palm Jumeirah
photographs
Papua New Guinea
photographs
particular others 52-53
parts of speech
See also names of specific parts of
speech
pathos 138
in investigative report 138
Paula (Allende) 103
PBS NewsHour 139
peer review 138
peers 48-49
perception 51

labels 51
personal identity 45, 46-48, 47, 48-49,
    50-51, 51, 54-56, 55, 66-67
    attachment styles and 47
        Figure
    by gender 11-12
    case study 66-67
    culture and 51, 54-56
    family influence of 45, 46-48
    peer influence on 48-49
    racial 11-12
    self-fulfilling prophecy in 8
    sexual orientation and 55
    society's influence on 50-51
    socioeconomic class and 12-13
personal relationships.
    See also romantic relationships
perspective 52-56
    internalization of 52-56
    see also social perspectives
Pew Research Center 111, 113-117,
    139
Phillips, Trevor 36, 39
Plaza del Potro
    photographs
position argument
    See also argument
Potomac River
    photographs
Prasad, Sunand 39
pronunciation 70-75
Prostitution.
    See also Slavery
PSAs.
    See public service announcements
    (PSAs)

punctuation
    See also names of specific
        punctuation marks
purpose.
    See rhetorical purpose "Queen of
        Mold, The" (Reichl)
Pyay
    photographs

Q

Quest for Truth: Scientific Progress
    and Religious Beliefs (Singham)
    120
quotations 136-137
    as support for logos 136-137

R

race 54-55, 56
    gender and 56
    personal identity from 54-55
    socioeconomic class and 13
    see also ethnocentrism
Rat runs 35
reasoning, soundness of
    See also rhetorical fallacies
reflected appraisal 53
research
    see also evidence
response.
    See fitting response
rhetorical appeals 137
rhetorical audience.
    See audience
rhetorical methods of development
    124, 129, 130, 136, 137, 142
    argument 136

cause-and-effect analysis 124, 130
classification and division 129
definition 22, 29, 142
description 29
exemplification 22, 137
rhetorical opportunity 109-110, 134-
    135
    identifying (activity) 109-110, 134-
        135
roles 57
    social 57
Rosen, Christine 109, 130-133
Rulfo, Juan 105
Russia
    photographs
Ruth, Babe 59

S

Salento, Colombia
    photographs
Salerno, Steve 50
Saving the Fish From Drowning (Tan)
    76
Sea bass 40
Sea Peoples
    photographs
secure attachment style 46
self-acceptance 61
self-change 58, 59-60, 60-61, 61
    acceptance for 61
    commitment to 58
    context for 18-19
    disclosure 60-61
    goals for 59-60
    knowledge for 15-16
self-concept.

See personal identity
self-disclosure 60-61
self-fulfilling prophecy 51
Self-Help (Smiles) 50
self-sabotage 62
self. 45, 51-52, 52-56, 58-62
    as process 9, 15
    defined 45
    development of 2
    enhancement of 58-62
    internalization for 52-56
    multidimensionality of 51-52
    See also personal identity
    See also personal identity
    self-change
sexual orientation 45, 55, 56, 57
    heterosexuality 45
    marriage and 57
    personal identity and 55
    socioeconomic class and 56
SHAM (Salerno) 50
Shepherd, Daniel 35
Shepherd, John 34-35
Silent Generation 110, 111
Silt
    photographs
Singham, Mano 120-123
Skellig Michael monastery
    photographs
slides
    Table
Smiles, Samuel 50
social communities.
    See also culture
social comparison 48
social networking.

See Facebook
See Facebook
Twitter
social perspectives 52-53, 54-56, 57
    changeability of 57
    construction of 14
    evolution of 14
    generalized other 54-56
    particular others 52-53
socioeconomic class 55-56, 56
    gender and 56
    personal identity and 55-56
    race and 13
    sexual orientation and 13
speeches to entertain.
    See entertaining speeches
speeches to persuade.
    See persuasive speaking
Spoken Here: Travels Among
    Threatened Languages (Abley) 91
statistics 137
STDs.
    See sexually transmitted diseases
    (STDs)
stereotypes 86
style
    CMS
    CMS
    MLA
    CMS
    MLA
    See also APA
    CMS
    MLA
    See also APA
    mechanics

T

Talking Power: The Politics of
    Language in Our Lives (Lakoff) 87
Tan, Amy 76-82
Tandy, Jessica 70
Taxi boats
    photographs
Taxis in New York
    photographs
television.
    See mass media
Thant, Than Swe
    photographs
The Biggest Loser (TV program) 50
The Bonesetter's Daughter (Tan) 76
The Faith Healer of Olive Avenue
    (Munoz) 70
The House of the Spirits (Allende) 103
The Hundred Secret Senses (Tan) 76
The Joy Luck Club (Tan) 76
The Kitchen God's Wife (Tan) 76
The Language of War (Lakoff) 87
The Opposite of Fate (Tan) 76
The Sum of Our Days (Allende) 103
The Swan (TV program) 50
Thompson, Derek 118-119
Tun Thein (transvestite)
    photographs
Tuxtla Gutierrez, Chipas, Mexico
    photographs

U

Union Jack 35

V

Varginha, Brazil
   photographs
Vittachi, Nury 92

W
Warsaw, Poland
   photographs
Williams, Neil 36
   photographs
women. 55, 57
   rights of 55, 57
   socialized role of 14
   See also femininity
Worrall, Simon 31-42

Z
Zigzagger (Munoz) 70
Zorro (Allende) 103

"
"Bad Student Writing? Not So Fast!"
   (Fendrich) 127-128
"downers," 62
"Last of the Music Videos, The"
   (Mayer) 140-142
"Leave Your Name at the Border"
   (Munoz) 70-75
"Lingua Franchise" (Foran) 90-94
"London on a Roll," 31-42
"Look at How Gen Y Communicates,
   A" (Fallarme) 124-125
"Millennial Muddle, The" (Hoover) 113
"Millennials, The: Confident.
   Connected. Open to Change."
   (Pew Research Center) 113-117
"More than Millennials: Teachers Must

Look Beyond Generational
   Stereotypes" (Singham) 120-123
"Mother Tongue" (Tan) 76-82
"Multilingual America" (Frey) 94-102
"Mute in an English-Only World" (Lee)
   83-86
"Myth of Multitasking, The" (Rosen)
   130-133
"Reading the History of the World"
   (Allende) 102-106
"The Power of Words in Wartime"
   (Lakoff) 87-90
"uppers," 62
"vultures," 62
"What's Really the Matter with 20-
   Somethings" (Thompson) 118-119
"Why Gen-Y Johnny Can't Read Non-
   Verbal Cues" (Bauerlein) 126-127